KAPPIYA'S HISTORICAL LEGENDS- 1

ALEXANDER THE GREAT

KAPPIYA CLASSICS

Contents

Foreword   *v*

  1. Introduction   1

  2. Alexander's Birthday   5

  3. Alexander's Boyhood And Youth   7

  4. Children Of Alexander Iii The Great   9

  5. Internet Myths & Trivia   13

  6. Coinage In Philip And Alexander's Time   20

  7. Transcendence   27

  8. Alexander's 'pothos'   29

  9. Alexander Quotes   31

10. Short Timeline   33

11. Detailed Timeline   37

12. Animals   44

13. Alexander In Art And Legend   53

14. Great Battles & Campaigns   67

15. Death   96

16. Religion   108

17. Sex   114

Foreword

KAPPIYA CLASSICS

Hello Dear Readers

I am Tamizhiniya Tamizhdesan

when I was studying in school my teachers used to conduct lessons between many good books and that conduct gave me confidence that I can conduct more than a hundred topics with introductory speech. My Technical education helped a lot in this aspect. When I became a teacher I assisted my students in the way our teachers guided us.

My school, college and workplace friends lives scattered in different countries like the poem of Eelam Poet V.I.S. Jayapalan, the families of them too scattered in different nation, whereas I live in the Land of my Mother Language(Tamilnadu). Among my friends who are running to strive for their living, I have selected the publishing department to read their lives and pass it on to others. We are publishing legendary works under Kappiya Vasipagam. So far we have published more than 1500 books in package type.

I have used the library a lot in my school, college and work life. Novelist Vasu Murugavel writes that he brought a bundle of books from a person, read them and returned them. Similarly, I have imported hundreds of books read them and sent them back. I have also written novel in Tamil and English, also a book based on the Culture of Tamil People.

My son Imayakappiyan (8) started learning his Tamil lettering from the texts of our cover pages. The same way he is gaining the knowledge of book names, authors also the technical knowledge in publishing and helps us in many ways. My husband Tamizhdesan guides me about the packaging materials of the book contents and his creative thinking of book cover page makes me to create some unique cover pages. We three feel very happy to be in this field which makes us to learn continuously.

I take great pleasure in publishing many of the war stories I have been reading. Movements that fight for the people are viewed by populists as scumbags. An example of this is the Tiger movement, which was not only similar to a government but also created various departments and the personality within them. There is no doubt that writing and reading them as well will diversify you.

CHAPTER I

Introduction

Who was Alexander? And why should he deserve to be called "the Great"?

On the throne

Alexander was born in 356 BC in Macedonia, the area around present day Thessaloniki in northern Greece. Though the Macedonians might have considered themselves part of the Greek cultural world, the other Greeks might have viewed them as half-barbarians. Alexander's father, King Philip, was an energetic ruler who had started a systematic policy of expanding his kingdom. Philip's main conquest was that of the Greek mainland, after his victory at Chaeronea in 338 BC. Alexander, still in his teens, commanded the Macedonian cavalry during this battle.

In 336 BC King Philip was killed and Alexander ascended to the throne of Macedonia. Within the next twelve years Alexander conquered almost the entire known world of his era. Though Alexander made use of the well-oiled army created by his father, he pushed the limits of Macedonian & Greek power to levels King Philip could not have dreamed of.

Persian foe

Alexander's main opponent was the Persian King Darius III. The Persian kingdom was an empire of epic proportions - stretching from Egypt and the Mediterranean into India and central Asia - which had dominated the ancient world for over two centuries. Most sources claim King Darius commanded incredibly huge armies. One million Persians are said to have taken the field against Alexander in 331 BC.

Alexander defeated Darius during three major engagements. In 334 BC he swept away a Persian defence force, sent by King Darius, at the river Granicus (Turkey). In 333 BC Darius faced the invader in person near the town of Issus (southern Turkey), but suffered a massive defeat. Alexander's brilliant final victory, at Gaugamela (Iraq) in 331 BC, irrevocably changed the course of history.

Edges of the earth

The capitals of Persia were now in Alexander's hands and he gained possession of the unbelievable gold reserves of the former Great Kings. However, Alexander and his army marched ever further eastward, battling nomadic warriors and rebels on the north-eastern fringes of the known world. In 326 BC he defeated King Porus at the river Hydaspes (India). But after this major, though difficult victory his troops refused to continue their conquests and Alexander finally ordered the return to his new capital Babylon.

During the 'retreat' many of his men perished in disastrous desert marches. Those who returned safely with Alexander had covered over 20,000 miles within a period of roughly ten years. In June 323 BC, back in Babylon, Alexander fell ill and died after ten days of high fever. Though his first wife Roxane was pregnant with her first son, Alexander the Great left no heir.

Leadership

So, why does he deserve the title "the Great"? Alexander was surely not the first person in history who got this title. The Persian King Cyrus the Great and the Egyptian Pharaoh Ramses the Great went before him. But it is recorded that even in Antiquity the Roman emperors already knew Alexander as "the Great".

The first clue is Alexander's leadership. Military experts still consider him one of the most outstanding commanders ever. Arguably, there is no one else in history who could inspire and motivate his men like Alexander did. Many explanations have been suggested: he suffered the same wounds as his soldiers, he payed attention to every single man in the army and he always led the attack in person. (Actually, he was the last great commander in history to take this personal risk.)

But apart from all that there must have been a deciding factor that we can only marvel about: charisma. Alexander was the only individual whose personal authority could hold his huge empire together. After his death it almost immediately fell apart into competing kingdoms. In 332 BC, in

Egypt, the famous oracle of Siwa allegedly confirmed that Alexander had divine origins and that the god Zeus (Ammon) was his true father. We do not know how Alexander himself thought about his divinity, but it surely helped him to boost the myth around his person.

Changing world

Alexander ranks among figures like Jesus Christ and Napoleon in the category "individuals who shaped the world as we know it". Before Alexander world civilisation had been dominated by eastern cultures - Persians, Egyptians, Babylonians. Alexander shifted the spotlight once and for all. From now on the western societies of the Romans and the Greeks would take over the torch.

Alexander had started to mint the gold reserves of the Persian kings and used his resources to continue his conquests and to build new cities and ports. Greek civilisation spread around the known world, improving trade relations and economic activities. The economic system that began to take shape after Alexander's reign remained virtually unchanged until the Industrial Revolution of the late 18th century.

Above that, Alexander had set the limits of what was considered the inhabited earth. It would last until the voyages of the Portugese and Spanish, in the late 15th century, before Europeans were convinced that they had finally explored further than Alexander had done.

God or devil?

Alexander's empire was no rosegarden. Especially after the final defeat of King Darius the court was plagued by controversy and intrigue. Alexander had some of his loyal aides tortured and killed. The justification for these acts is still subject to debate. Especially during the campaign in India, the Macedonians used brutal force to subdue the conquered peoples. Even the sick and elderly, it is written, were butchered. But also earlier on, during the long siege of Tyre (Lebanon) in 332 BC, Alexander had 2,000 inhabitants mercilessly crucified. In modern Iran he is still known as an evil king - a personification of the devil if you like - who did his very best to destroy the respectable old Persian culture and religion.

On the other hand some western scholars have presented Alexander as a visionary who believed in the peaceful co-existance of different nations and races within his empire. They refer - for example - to mass-weddings ordered by Alexander to reconciliate Greeks and Persians. In the Middle Ages his figure had evolved into a legendary hero, the quintessential example of chivalry and worldly power. In our present time, as he had a lifelong relationship with his comrade Hephaistion, he has been portrayed as a "gay hero".

It is still very difficult to view his personality without being biased one way or the other

The Sources

How do we know so much about him?

"The Greatest Legend of All Was Real"

He was. His original name was Alexandros Philippou Makedonon (Alexander son of Philip of Macedon) and he lived from 356 BCE to 323 BCE. As the third king of Macedonia bearing this name, he is also referred to as Alexander III.

About 99% of what we know about Alexander the Great comes to us through five original sources from Antiquity whose ancient works have somehow survived the ages in various more or less complete manuscripts: Arrian, Plutarch, Curtius, Diodorus and Justin. Some might like to add the late Antiquity Metz Epitome to these Big Five.

The works of Arrian, Plutarch and Curtius are still highly readable and readily available in modern translations. It is even said that Jim Morrison of The Doors read Plutarch's "Life of Alexander".

CHAPTER II

Alexander's Birthday

Sources

The Greek writer Plutarch, who wrote his "Life of Alexander" around 100 A.D., is practically our only source concerning the birth of Alexander the Great and its circumstances. As this is only one piece of information, its value tends to be relative. Knowledge starts when you have the same piece of information from different, independent sources. So one has to bear in mind that whatever Plutarch says could be only legend and might not be backed up by other sources.

Artemis

The British scholar Nicholas Hammond made a thorough analysis of the probable dating of Alexander's birth in his "Sources for Alexander the Great" (Cambridge, 1993). Hammond shows that Plutarch probably got his date of 6th of the Attic month Hecatombaeon 356 B.C. for Alexander's birthday from a contemporary writer, Timaeus, who was also born in 356 B.C. Plutarch says Alexander was born on the same day that the Temple of Artemis at Ephesus (near Izmir in modern Turkey) was destroyed by fire. Artemis was, amongst her other attributes, the goddess of childbirth. Legend had it that this destruction by fire of this shrine (which eventually became one of the famous Seven Wonders of the ancient world) spelled doom for the peoples of Asia. There is a possibility that the dating of Alexander's birth has been manipulated by our ancient sources to coincide with this disaster. See also: Seven Wonders.

20th of July?

So, author Robin Lane Fox cites three possibilities for Alexander's birthday: July 20th 356 B.C. or thereabouts, July the 6th 356 B.C. or October 356 B.C. Basically, Cicero gives essentially the same story about Alexander's birth and the temple of Ephesus burning down as Plutarch does, and he too attributes it to Timaeus. It follows that the date of 6th of Hecatombaeon is well-sourced. Unfortunately, it is difficult to match this date exactly with the Julian Calendar (which we tend to use for ancient events). Hammond says there is general agreement for the second half of July. So, after all, **20th of July** is a good guess.

Legends

Of course, Alexander's birth became surrounded by other legends as well. Stories circulated around the Macedonian court that his mother Olympias had conceived from a snake. Olympias had startling dreams too --- about a circle of fire extending to the outer reaches of the earth. And also there is a dream of King Philip II about Olympias' womb being sealed by a lion.

Body & Height

Arrian said he was somewhat less than average height, Curtius that he was not of impressive physique and/or stature. Existing art shows him to be muscular with good length of leg and somewhat stocky, so Curtius must be referring to his height. What was average height back then? Macedonians, who had access to grazing land, probably ate better and were likely taller than the Southern Greeks. Some scholars speculate that the armor found in Tomb II [Vergina, Macedonia/Greece; see picture] must be either Alexander's or Philip's. The armor would have fit a person of 5' 2" or shorter. Both Kings were not popular with the writing Greeks, and I find it hard to believe such a lack of height would not have been mentioned by contemporaries. The armor probably belonged to Arrhidaeous' wife, whose own mother would have been a warrior herself and raised her daughter to be one. Alexander was an excellent warrior. A lack of height this extreme would have put him at a severe disadvantage as a soldier, particularly on foot, due to leverage considerations with weapons and shields. And Alexander battled often on foot, not always on horseback.

The expert on Alexander Art, Andrew Stewart, places his height at 5'7" which is very close to my own estimate of 5'6" - just short enough to be noticed, but not to be disadvantageous and not worthy of mention in contemporary writings by authors who would have ran about the same height. In later times, where great stature was synonymous with great deeds, people wondered why a King so remarkable in all other things was not distinguished in that one area which was so a reflection of a gift from the Gods.

CHAPTER III

Alexander's Boyhood and Youth

We actually know very little about Alexander's childhood. Plutarch was the only author who wrote about it, and he was concerned only with events that exemplified Alexander's character. It is therefore difficult to separate, even in Plutarch's short section on this period of his life, the apocryphal from the true. However, we can make certain assumptions based on what we know about life for Greek children in general.

Alexander would have spent the first few years of his life in the women's quarters, where Olympias would have laid the groundwork for the influence she later clearly exerted on her son. Later he was put into the care of tutors, who were responsible for overseeing his education—in the early stages, learning to read and write. These tutors included Leonidas, one of Olympias' kinsmen, who was infamous for his spartan ways (Pl. Alex. 5.4; also). Another tutor was Lysimachus, who was at least partly responsible for Alexander's identification with Achilles (Pl. Alex. 5.5).

It is likely that Alexander was thrown together with his 'syntrophoi' at a fairly early age. Boys such as Hephaestion, Perdiccas, Leonnatus, and Seleucus would have received their education alongside the prince. They then followed him to Mieza, at the age of around 14, when Aristotle became their tutor. We do not know exactly what was on Aristotle's curriculum, but it seems certain that literature, mathematics, history, philosophy and natural history were all taught at Mieza. As these were the boys' teenage years, they would also at this time have been taught the arts of war—they undoubtedly already rode well, and now will have practised wrestling, running, discus and javelin throwing; and will also probably have taken part in phalanx manoeuvres.

Plutarch tells one or two stories about Alexander's youth. The most famous is probably the story of Alexander's taming of Bucephalus, when he was around 13 years old (Pl. Alex. 6). Another well-known story is that of Alexander's meeting with the Persian ambassadors (Pl. Alex. 5.1-3)—Philip was absent from the court when the ambassadors arrived, and Alexander kept them amused by asking precocious questions about the Great King's empire.

The final stage in the boys' education will have been as members of the corps of Royal Pages, which was a sort of cadet force, answerable only to the king. Alexander appears not to have served much time as a true Page, as he was already regent of Macedonia at the age of 16, and two years later commanded the cavalry at Chaeronea. By the time that Alexander was made regent, albeit temporarily, his youth was over. He led a military expedition against the Maedi and founded his first city (or, rather, re-named the existing Maedi settlement) (Pl. Alex. 9.1-2). After that it is unlikely that any would have presumed him still to be a boy. However, his clashes with Philip, most notably over the Pixodarus affair (probably when he was about 18/19), show that he was still considered a hot-headed youth in some respects, and that he had not yet achieved the maturity of political thought that Philip had had to gain at an early age, and which Alexander himself would have to learn very quickly, not long afterwards (Pl. Alex. 10.1-3).

CHAPTER IV

Children of Alexander III the Great

'Confirmed' Children of Alexander

Herakles

The first child of Alexander was Herakles, son of Alexander's mistress Barsine. Barsine was the widow of Memnon, the prominent Greek mercenary general serving under the Persian King Darius III. She was the daughter of the Persian satrap Artabazus. Barsine was captured by Parmenion in Damascus, in late 333 BC, shortly after the battle of Issus. Barsine had traveled with the Persian army from Babylon to the Mediterranean but went to Damascus before the battle.

According to Diodorus Herakles was 17 years of age when he died in 309 BC. This implies that Herakles was born in 326-327 BC during the Indian campaign. When Alexander died in 323 BC Herakles is reported to have lived in Pergamon, in western Asia Minor, together with his mother.

There is no further mention of him in the sources until he is summoned to Europe by Polyperchon in 309 BC, after the death of Alexander IV. (According to Justin Herakles and Barsine stayed in Pydna, Macedonia.) The army started to show some interest in Herakles, as he was the last remaining member of Alexander's Argead house. So Cassander persuaded Polyperchon to murder him. Herakles was apparently strangled after a banquet. Barsine was murdered too. Their bodies, according to Justin, were buried privately to conceal the plot.

Our source Justin raises some confusion about Herakles' age and date of birth by saying that he was 14 when he died, which should put his date of birth around 324 BC. Justin has probably mistaken Herakles' age with that of Alexander IV.

Alexander IV

Alexander's second child was Alexander IV, son of Alexander's first wife Roxane. Roxane was the daughter of Persian nobleman Oxyartes, a local ruler in Sogdiana who surrendered to Alexander during the siege of the Sogdian Rock. Alexander is said to have fallen in love with Roxane at first sight. The marriage was arranged in spring or August of 327 BC. The motives for the marriage, however, certainly had a political context too. Some references claim Roxane was only 12 at the time, but there is no evidence for that.

When Alexander died in June 323 BC Roxane was either six (Curtius) or eight (Justin) months pregnant. The newborn infant Alexander IV was recognized as king-to-be, formally sharing kingship with Alexander's halfbrother Arrhidaeus for the time being. Antipater, Alexander's regent in Macedonia, brought Alexander IV and his mother Roxane to Macedonia. After Antipater's death the new regent Polyperchon placed Olympias, Alexander's mother, in charge of Alexander IV.

In 316 BC Cassander took over power in Macedonia. Grandma Olympias was eliminated in 315 BC. Cassander put Roxane and Alexander IV under guard of his aide Glaucias, in Amphipolis, and removed all signs of Royal status from the child. Alexander IV and his mother were finally killed by Glaucias on orders of Cassander, probably in 310 BC. It is relevant to note that although Babylonian sources indeed mention Arrhidaeus as Alexander's Royal successor, they never refer to the infant kingship of Alexander IV.

'Other' Children of Alexander

Roxane's first child

The Metz Epitome, a late Antiquity source, mentions a first child of Alexander and Roxane, that is supposed to have been born at the Indus in 326 BC, and died soon after birth.

"There he found the ships which Porus and Taxiles had built, 800 biremes and 300 store-ships, and he put on board crews and provisions. In the meantime Alexander's son by Roxane died." (Metz Epitome, 70.)

Queen Cleophis' son

Alexander is said to have conceived a child with the Indian Queen Cleophis of Massaga, now in northern Pakistan. Our source for this is Justin. Cleophis is said to have achieved by sexual favours what she could not achieve by force of arms, and her son Alexander rose to sovereignty over the Indians. However: "Queen Cleophis was from that time called the 'royal whore' by the Indians." (Justin, 12.7.11.)

There are other tales of Alexander fathering children on Indian princesses. The Malay annals have him fathering a son on Shahru'l-Bariyah, daughter of Raja Kida Hindi. The son is left behind in India as Alexander has long since gone.

Queen Statira's child

Queen Statira, wife of Darius III, was captured by Alexander at Issus in 333 BC. She is said to have died in childbirth before the battle of Gaugamela in 331 BC. (Plutarch, 30.) The question is: when exactly? Arrian tries to convice his readers that Alexander never touched 'the most beautiful woman' in Asia. However, if Statira died later than spring 332 BC, there is a slight chance that she might have carried Alexander's child, not the child of Darius. We will never know.

'No' Children of Alexander

Princess Statira's pregnancy

Alexander married to princess Statira, daughter of Darius III and Queen Statira, in Susa in 324 BC. She had been captured at Issus, together with her mother and sister. Soon after Alexander's death in 323 BC Statira was murdered by Roxane and Perdiccas. Nothing in the sources suggests that Statira was pregnant at that time.

Thalestris, the Amazon Queen

Our classic sources seem to confirm - or suggest - that Alexander spent thirtheen nights with Thalestris, the Queen of the legendary female Amazon warriors. This is supposed to have happened around 330BC/329 BC, near the shores of the Caspian. Thalestris begged Alexander to conceive a child with her. It did not happen.

Grandchildren of Alexander

Alexander the Great had no grandchildren. The only two 'confirmed' children of Alexander, Herakles and Alexander IV, were murdered before adulthood.

CHAPTER V

Internet Myths & Trivia

Here is your overview of modern myths that are apparently taken serious by many, but are - most likely - just the result of the rise of the Internet.

The emergence of the world wide web has given a real boost to the creation of new myths about Alexander. As pothos.org visitor Amyntoros remarked on November 7th 2003: "There were two sisters in the US who have written advice columns for decades - Ann Landers and Dear Abby. Whenever there are any letters written regarding epilepsy or being left-handed, Alexander is included in the lists of famous people in the response. The columnists use information from related organizations on the two subjects - but as to where *they* got the info, well that's another matter. But these two women have probably been read by more people than anyone else in the world - I kid you not - and unless challenged, their information is considered *gospel*."

Epilepsy

In 2003 an article in The Times stated that Alexander was epileptic. UK television host Stephen Fry repeated that statement on the IQ Quiz Show. Alexander is frequently mentioned in lists of celebrities with epilepsy. But our historical sources contain no clues whatsoever to back up this claim. (Julius Caesar might have suffered from epilepsy, as well as Alexander's half-brother Philip Arrhidaeus. But not Alexander.)

Left-handedness

A common myth: Alexander should have been left-handed. We have all heard it, but there is no historical source.

Hair Dye

The only Alexanders known to have dyed their hair are Colin Farrell and Richard Burton.

Cats

Alexander is supposed to have hated cats. You can find this myth all over the Internet. Plutarch (100 A.D.) mentions Alexander had a dog that he was very fond of. But none of our sources mentions even the slightest reference to cats. (Oh, except for lions, which Alexander hunted.)

Alexander the Diabetic

The myth that Alexander was a diabetic has even been copied by scholars and can be found in various books. Again, no evidence in our historical sources.

He Was Gay!

Well, not in the modern sense. The Ancients did not have the same approach to sexuality as modern man. Alexander married to three women (Roxane, Statira and Parysatis), he had a lifelong (love) relationship with his boyhood friend Hephaistion, he had at least one mistress (Barsine) and he might have had an (erotic) affection towards Bagoas the eunuch (a castrated man). Why not read the excellent Sexuality article by Jeanne Reames-Zimmerman?

Mystical Grandchildren

As far as we have evidence from our Ancient sources, Alexander had no grandchildren. His few known children were eliminated at a very young age during the successor wars. Buy yes, those mystical grandchildren are being invented and re-invented everytime someone wants to claim some kind of relation to, or descent from, Alexander. Indeed, there are several families claiming Alexander the Great as an "ancestor", going so far as to put their "family trees" on the Internet... Grandiose ancestral tales, no doubt.

African Safari

Some tales published on the web refer to Alexander as the ancestor of the Turkana tribe, living in the semi-deserts of northern Kenya. It is even claimed that the Turkana themselves see Alexander as their founding father.

Pothos.org invites any proud Turkana visitor to this site to confirm this - but I have my strong doubts. This myth fits in perfectly with a long-standing tradition that denies sub-Saharan Africans the ability to achieve anything on their own account. Romantic historians have argued that the Maasai people in Kenya and Tanzania are in fact the descendants of a lost Roman legion. The majestic ruins of Great Zimbabwe in southern Africa were once attributed to King Solomon. The early 20th century Somali fortress of Taleh was thought to have been build by the Ancient Egyptians. Get the picture?

Alexander Was a Freemason

This goes back to the legend of Alexander visiting Jerusalem. There is a sign used in Freemasonry which was "used by Moses" when he came down the from the mount. When Alexander approached Jerusalem he was met by the High Priest who saluted him with this significant sign. "It is a historical fact that Alexander was so much struck with the sight of this procession that he did homage to Gods vice-regent, and it is said, on more questionable authority, that his reverence proceeded from the mutual recognition of the Masonic Brotherhood."

There is also a very high order in the Freemasons known as the Synods of the Ancient and Heroic Order of the Gordian Knot!

The Philosopher's Stone or Emerald Tablet of Alchemy

This myth seems to have originated in medieval records supposedly written by Albertus Magnus though they are believed to be spurious. "Central to the mysteries of alchemy was the belief that ancient texts contained forgotten secrets of nature. The most definitive of these texts was the Tabula Smaragdina or Emerald Tablet, which, according to legend, had been discovered by Alexander the Great in the Egyptian tomb of Hermes Trismegistos ('thrice-great'), the Greek counterpart of the Egyptian god of wisdom and magic, Thoth. The Emerald Tablet was inscribed with thirteen axioms. Unfortunately, they were rather difficult to understand. The riddle-like language of the fourth is typical: 'Its father is the sun, its mother the moon; the wind carries it in its belly, its nurse is the earth'. This cryptic style was emulated by the alchemists, who christened themselves sons of Hermes' or Hermetic philosophers." Another version of the legend suggests that Alexander the Great found the Tabula Smaragdina in the Great Pyramid of Cheops.

Alexander mythology persisted through the entire Near East literally for hundreds of years after his death, and legends of earlier heroes have been subsumed into his mythos: for instance, both Alexander and the Sumerian hero Gilgamesh were supposed to have found the fountain (or rose) of immortality somewhere under the ocean, and both were supposedly unable to bring it back to mankind - foiled by the depth of the waters which kept the treasure safe. Though Alexander's existence is far more documented than (for instance) that of King Arthur, exactly the same sort of folk mythology circulated about both men."

Another quote from Magnus, but the URL has been taken down. "The always victorious Alexander the Great wore a chrysoprase stone in his girdle. One day a snake bit off the girdle and dropped it in the river. From that time forward Alexander never won another battle." (Presumably, these battles were ones fought after Alexander died, as he never lost one in his lifetime!)

The Secret of Secrets

Francis Bacon became immensely interested in a pseudo-Aristotelian text, "Secretum secretorum" (Secret of Secrets), which is thought to have been written by Aristotle for Alexander the Great, his pupil, on kingship. This pseudo-Aristotelian text was one of the most widely read books of the Middle Ages and there were different versions. The first was introduced to medieval Europe by the translator John of Seville in Toledo (Spain) around 1130. The text contained a lot of ethic questions and occult lore ranging from astrology to the magical properties of plants, gems, and numbers, as well as a strange account of a unified science. According to the text, only a person with the proper moral and intellectual background could discover this unified science.

Palmistry

"The ancient Greeks were keen traders and it is believed that palmistry spread there from India. Aristotle wrote on the subject in De Historia Animalium more than 2,500 years ago. Alexander the Great had Aristotle write a book for him on the subject."

Aloe Vera

"Greek and Roman physicians such as Dioscorides and Pliny the Elder used it (Aloe Vera) to great effect and legend suggests that Aristotle persuaded Alexander the Great to capture the island of Socotra in the Indian Ocean to get its rich supply of aloe to heal his wounded soldiers."

Chess

"According to myths persisting to this day, the origin of the game of chess is shrouded in the midst of time. Ever since an archaeologist brought to light a 6,000-year-old Greek manuscript apparently depicting a chessboard, there has been many an overzealous historian eager to date the play of this game to the days of Methuselah. However, modern research suggests that the so-called 'chess board' represented nothing more than a run of the mill battle plan. Today, it is believed that the inspiration for the game dates back to the year 326 BC when Alexander the Great massed his army at the gates of the Orient. Opposing him, stood the four divisions of the Hindu army: chariots, elephants, cavalry and infantry. Almost 1,000 years passed before someone thought to immortalize this memorable battle as a diversion reserved for the rich and powerful."

The Indians Had Firearms!

In the preface to a Code of Gentoo Laws or Ordinations of the Pundits: From a Persian translation, made from the original, written in the Shanscrit language, occurs the following passage: "It will no doubt strike the reader with wonder to find a prohibition of firearms in records of such unfathomable antiquity; and he will probably from hence renew the suspicion which has long been deemed absurd, that Alexander the Great did absolutely meet with some weapons of that kind in India as a passage in Quintus Curtius seems to ascertain. Gunpowder has been known in China, as well as in Hindustan, far beyond all periods of investigation."

It is interesting to note that the same is mentioned by Francis Bacon in one of his essays. He is even more specific, mentioning the Oxydracae as the owners of the guns.

Close Encounters

In the US the A&E's Ancient Mysteries television series has claimed that Alexander saw flying "silver shields" in the sky when he embarked on his campaign to Asia and when he was besieging Tyre. It seems just a matter of time before the first story about Alexander's alleged alien abduction will appear.

True Love

Alexander's one true love should have been a woman called Melissa. Who ever made that up? There is no personality called Melissa in any of the sources.

Snakes

Alexander slept with snakes? This new myth has its origins somewhere in the fiction books of Mary Renault.

Panic Disorder

Apart from epilepsy, left-handedness, diabetic symptoms and fear of cats - according to author Doherty Alexander had a "panic disorder" too, whatever that means.

Alexander Died of Syphilis!

We always suspected this! Quote: "But Alexander was ultimately defeated by epilepsy, syphilis and madness. As his illness progressed, he became more ambitious, greedy and cruel. Bouts of erratic and violent behavior replaced pragmatism. He killed one of his top advisers in a drunken brawl over a trinket or two at a party."

Leprosy

At last: A possible truth here? Hansen's Disease (leprosy) is a good example. This disfiguring bacterium probably originated in Egypt, spreading to India by 600 B.C. But leprosy was apparently unknown in Europe until the return of Alexander the Great's armies from India in 326 BC. Starting in Greece the bacterium rapidly spread throughout the continent. By the time of the Roman Empire leprosy was already considered ancient and was widely feared and discussed.

CHAPTER VI

Coinage in Philip and Alexander's time

Coinage on Philip; as Philip gained controll of Macedonia he also eventually gained control of all twenty four ancient cities including the invaluable mints. He began his royal coinage at Pella (358-356) shortly after came Amphipolis and so on. The island of Thasos retained its independence until at least 340, for it supported Byzantium against Philip in 340/39 and joined the League of Corinth in 338/7. After the siege of Byzantium by Philip in 340/39 a celebrated historical event I may add, Lee Rider, BCH LXXX (1956), p. 18, where he remarks that numismatic evidence now requires that scholars abandon the hypothesis that Philip conquered Thasos in 340 BCE.

A few precious metal coinages terminated by Philip's conquests, and others that survived for varying periods. Apart from the Chalcidian campaign there seems to be no correlation between the date a city came under Philip's control and the demise of its coinage. Yet most of these coinages did end during his lifetime. In several cases—Amphipolis, Philippi, and Maroneia—it appears that the coinage was partly co-opted to serve the ends of Philip's imperialism and was discontinued when its usefulness was exhausted. In each of these three cases the cessation of minting may be correlated with new operations elsewhere: royal silver was first struck at Pella when the Amphipolitan series wound up; the royal Macedonian gold coinage began shortly after the last gold issues of Philippi; and coining resumed at Abdera with the closure of the Maroneia mint. This system points to a royal monetary policy that evolved in piecemeal out of an earlier phase in which Philip opportunistically drew on civic mints and coinages. The cites which continued their coinage the longest period of time after falling into Philip's controll was Abdera and Thasos for they were very close to the precious metal deposits around Mt. Pangaeus.

Latter coinages of Abdera, Aenus, Maroneia, and Thasos displayed a difference in weight standard or in the size of denominations minted. In light of archaeological evidence, which shows the wine and agricultural trade continued to flourish; monumental public buildings continued to be constructed, but now they were financed by wealthy individuals rather than the state.

Philip was sagacious in adapting means to ends and the major ancient cities that were important to his consolidations with his new Macedonia coinage were; Abdera, Acanthus, Aeneia, Aenus, Amphipolis, Dicaea, Eion, Maroneia, Mende, Methone, Neapolis, Olynthus, Pella, Philippi (Crenides), Potidaea, Pydna, Saloniki (Thessalonica), Scione, Sermylia, Stageira, Thasos, Therme, Torone, and Tragilos.

Coinage on Alexander III; the kings money was struck in three metals and a variety of denominations, these were the most important: Gold Stater, obverse; head of Athena right in crested Corinthian helmet. Reverse; winged Nike standing left, holding wreath in right hand, stylis in left; Silver Tetradrachm, obverse; head of young Herakles right in lion's skin headdress. Reverse; Zeus seated left on throne, eagle on outstretched right hand, with left hand leaning on a long scepter. Bronze Unit, obverse; head of young Herakles right in lion's skin headdress. Reverse; bow in case and club. All these normally bear symbols on the reverse which distinguish the mints and issues.

After a decade or less of lavish expenditure, Philip at his death left a nearly empty treasury and possibly a debt as well to Alexander. Griffith, Greece and Rome 12 (1965) p. 127, perversely interprets this tradition as indicating merely that Philip's annual income was insufficient for the Asian campaign. Under Alexander the Amphipolis mint achieved a much greater output than under Philip.

Though Alexander continued to mint Philip's gold these types were by no means suited to the ambitious and soaring mind of Alexander, who therefore selected Pallas "the patroness of the besiegers of Ilium" and a war like Nike with a "trophy-stand." The curiosity of other scholars, however, has not been so easily satisfied, and a considerable literature has grown up about the identification of Pallas and Nike: Athena Promachus, Pheidias' heroic bronze statue which stood on the Acropolis between the Erechtheium and the Pyopylaea, a dedication, according to Pausanias, from the spoils of the Persians defeated at Marathon. It may be added that when Pallas appears on the obverse of Pella's own coins it is in the form of Athena Parthenus as a possible original from the ancient Palladium of Pella.

(I5.I) Plutarch quotes Aristobulus that on his crossing to Asia Alexander had only 70 talents in the war chest while Duris says it was provisions for 30 days and Onesicritus adds his debt was 200 talents besides. Curtius (X. II) said he inherited 60 talents along with a debt of 500, while Arrian gives the most extreme of all (VII.9.6): Philip's debt of 500 talents had increased by borrowing 800 more. If Philip's debt was a total of 1,300 talents this account would have been no problem. Interest at Athens ranged from 12% to 18%. If there was a yearly interest of 234 talents to pay the mines at Philippi alone yielded 1,000 talents.

If Alexander's army of invasion and Parmenio's advanced force was 40,000 foot and 6,000 horse (G.T. Griffith, The Mercenaries of the Hellenistic World, Cambridge, 1935, p. 12) it could not have been supported for 30 days on 70 talents. Unfortunately silence prevailed with the sources on the matter of the soldiers' daily wage in Alexander's army. However, we have a detailed proposal by Demosthenes (First Philippic, 28f.) for an expeditionary force against Philip that was never raised. His calculations allows 2 obols a day for foot soldiers, one drachma for horse, citizen and mercenary alike. By the time of Alexander the pay of a Greek mercenary was 4 obols a day and we may assume the pay of all privates was the same; in that case the pay for a horseman was also double Demosthenes' figure. Now the pay of the foot soldiers for 30 days would be 800,000 drachmae (40,000 x 4 obols x 30 days divided by 6), that of the horse 360,000 drachmae (6,000 x 12 obols x 30 days divided by 6). The total, one hundred ninety three and one third talents (1,160,000 divided by 6,000), even at Demosthenes' figures the sum would be ninety six and two thirds talents with no allowance for the pay of higher ranks or any other military expense. Therefore, seventy talents would not have lasted three weeks even at starvation wages.

At the time of Alexander's invasion of Asia the currency in the east consisted mostly of Persian gold darics and silver sigloi and Athenian tetradrachms. The gold darics and the Athenian tetradrachms enjoyed a world-wide circulation for the last hundred-fifty years and were well known and acceptable to Alexander's soldiers. From the battle of the Granikos to the invasion of India, for the pay of his troops he relied on principally upon the fabulous huge hoards of wealth which had been stored away by the Persian monarchs which now fell into his hands. Naturally Alexander would issue coins bearing his own name and types to take the place, as soon as possible, to a fast vanishing dynasty and empire. In fact his own coinage had already begun to appear in Macedonia, Thrace, and Asia Minor. Facilities were close at hand for him to issue his own coins nearer to the scenes of his immediate operations. His overthrow of the Persian power had interrupted the activities of the satrapal mints in Cilica and the autonomous mints of Arados, Byblos, Sidon, Tyre, and Gaza. In busy commercial centres and at important and convenient points Alexander had all the needed mints, appliances, and workmen for an immediate issue of his own coins. It is indeed natural that Alexander made great use of the Sidonian mint; in addition, it formed the principal base for the operations against Tyre. While large sums of money-more than enough to pay the soldiers for the present-had been captured at the battle of Issos (Arrian II, 11, at Issos 3000 talents; a still larger amount at Damaskos) and, later, at Damaskos, Alexander would not delay the appearance of a coinage bearing his own name and types.

Circa 325 -- 315 B.C

A very rare coin was produced in Pella, the head of young Herakles facing left in lion's headdress. The depiction of Heracles facing left is highly unusual clearly departing from the customary Alexandrine coinage and present only in coins from Macedonian mints. Scholars have variously explained such variations as experiments, similarly with the explanations in the very nations and Philip II coinage, Newell maintains that the departure from the original design might have been an experiment of a major mint most likely of Pella an important Macedonian mint but with a limited geographical circulation only a major mint could have afforded to introduce new, possibly unwelcome elements and their coin production without criticism. Price argues instead that perhaps the divergence in design was meant to mark the work of a part particular mint, perhaps a newly opened facility.

The next objective for Alexander was the mints at Babylon and Susa of course make no mistake the biggest prize of them all was Persepolis.

As you observed no army passed present or future can be successful without good logistics. Without logistics you have no army and without money you have no logistics, this is why Alexander was so successful because capturing the mints was his prime objective. Forgive me for I must stray to let it be known that all of Alexander's battles were important but the two most important battles were no doubt Gaugalmela and the battle for Persis. As most of us have known Gaugamela was a major battle and Persis was considered a minor battle but nonetheless the most important battle over all and allow me to explain; this battle to accurately conquer the Persian Empire and in a state of fear actually started at the Susian Gates.

The surtrap of Persepolis, Susa, and Babylon was an ingenious fellow by the name of Ariobarzanes. After the battle Gaugamela Ariobarzanes was furious of the outcome of the battle Gaugamela that he had no intentions of turning tail and run like the coward Darius the third. While Alexander was gloating with a swollen head Ariobarzanes rounded up all the Persian fighters he could find for an ingenious trap with good intelligence to eliminate Alexander for ever.

The battle for Persis

Arobarzanes was well prepared for any such advance and had made ready to ambush the invading forces. Using to his advantage wisely he had built a defense of wall across the narrow pass with artillery hidden behind it, and 40,000 infantry and 700 horse ranged along the ridges of the summit. The Macedonians were outnumbered by more than two to one; Alexander mounted a direct assault over the difficult rocky terrain, as they reach the narrow section of the past at that time Arobarzanes gave the order to attack and, using the catapults unleashed a barrage of rocks, arrows, and javelins. This immense firepower rained like a thunderstorm into the gorge to inflict huge casualties on Alexander's men; by leading his men into an ignorant and hopeless position Alexander realized his error and sounded a temporary retreat, hastily backing off down the gorge to a clearing 3 miles west. Furious with himself for having failed to foresee the possibility of a trap Alexander realized he must find an alternative route to the impenetrable way ahead and a means of avenging the fallen, in which their were many. Arrian is very clear about what happened to Craterus. By keeping many fires going all night he had orders to stay behind and guard the rear of the pass during Alexander's advance.

Many times Alexander would fall into the foulest smelling stench of stool and come out smelling like a rose and this event was no exception. However Alexander's luck continued: if they did not reach Persepolis in time not only the treasures could be lost, but Parmenio's column would be an easy slaughter to a Persian surprise attack. However, a local shepherd claimed there was an obscure mountain path around the gates. During the hours of darkness Alexander took his elite units on a nightly march moving blown down trees and rocks that would be stable on an unused pass, this nightly backpacking endeavor was quiet and fast. And believe me this shepherd boy was well rewarded.

To speed up his advance to Persepolis Alexander decided to divide his army at the point where the royal road branched south-East, sending

Parmenio and the heavy infantry and baggage train on the lower road across the plains through Shiraz. Alexander himself would leave a force of around 20,000 light-armed shock-troops across the snowy, frosted terrain Zagros Mountains and through the narrow 10km long pass of the Persian Gates. Alexander was prepared for touch resistance at the pass no doubt one of his biggest blunders of all of his campaign. According to Arrian Alexander took with him the Royal Agema squadron of the companions, another double squadron of Calvary, the guards (Hypaspists), Perdiccas' battalion, the Agrians and the most lightly armed of the archers. The battalions of Philotas, Coenus, and Amyntas received orders from Alexander to proceed in a different direction. Arrian also says Ptolemy had the command over 3000 troops.

Luck will beat skill any day and when you have skill and luck on your side you are unbeatable! With Alexander's plans of communiqui to Amyntas, Philotas, and Coenus with their three infantry brigades in position; Craterus and his men advance from the entrance of the gorge. Alexander supported by Ptolemy assembled at the back of the pass behind the Persian positions. Before the beginning of the dusk of dawn when the sky turns a dark blue and you can still see stars Amyntas, Philotas, and Coenus attacked with their brigades Craterus and his men advance from the entrance of the gorge as Alexander simultaneously launched his assault from behind the enemy lines continuing to battle a scream of vengeance. With Ariobarzanes already engaged on three fronts Alexander signaled Ptolemy and his 3000 infantry to attack down the gorge into the sides of the defenders were they were cut to pieces in intense hand-to-hand combat, luckily for Ariobarzanes he was able to escape with a few others on horseback but for the rest of his men the battle was complete carnage in its purest form. There would be no military honors given the enemy in this battle for their bodies were mutilated to un-recognition. Ariobarzanes returned to Persepolis before Alexander arrived, only to be denied entrance to the city. News of the outcome of the battle had convinced the citadel commander of Persepolis to surrender the capital to Alexander. Ariobarzanes had no choice but to get out of Dodge and completely disappeared from the face of the earth.

When Alexander arrived to Persepolis it was one of the most beautiful citadels he had ever seen but more important the treasure was all intact. Imagine diamonds, silver, gold, and emeralds as large as footballs (uncut). Did I mention the huge talents of coinage?

Diodorus says that the capture of Susa brought in 40,000 talents of uncoiled gold and silver and 9000 talents of darics; that of Persepolis, 120,000 talents reckoning the gold added value in silver. Arrian (III.. I6. 7) Susa 50,000 talents, Persepolis, 120,000 talents. Curtius (V. 2. II; 6. 9). Susa, 50,000 talents, Persepolis, 120,000 talents. Plutarch, (Alex., 36. I; 37. 2) Susa 40,000 talents coined, Persepolis an equal amount of coin. Justin (XL. 14. 9) Susa 40,000 talents, Persepolis 120,000 coin.

In 1975 a movie was made called The "Man Who Would Be King" based on a short story by Rudyard Kipling, adapted and filmed by John Houston in 1975 along with Michael Caine and Sean Connery. This movie has similarities and it was slightly about Alexander the great. For a brief moment it showed a small portion of Alexander's treasure and this small treasure was massive.

CHAPTER VII

Transcendence

Alexander's greatest passion can be expressed simply as: transcendence.

Arrian states it accurately if mundanely: "if there had been no other competition, he would have competed against himself" (7.1). If he had aimed just to outdo his father, he'd have limited himself to outdoing his father, and lost his motivation after conquering more territory than his father ever had. He wanted to surpass every limit, within or without, to be larger than life and more than human, like the ancient heroes. He wanted to transcend the possible, as witness the many times he was told he couldn't do something, but did it nonetheless.

He wanted to transcend his nationality, to expand himself to incorporate the cultures of his subjects, which got him into trouble with the old-guard Makedonians. He wanted to transcend the very concept of nations and states by conquering the world.

Small size colossus

Small of stature, he wanted to transcend his size, and be seen as a colossus. He wanted to transcend any previous mental limits of scale: to come up with the greatest strategy, tactics and logistics, to hold the richest banquet, have the largest wedding, enable the most active trade and prosperity, lead the bravest and most skilled army, build the greatest empire, enable the best scientific knowledge, give the most expensive gifts, and so on -- that the world had ever seen.

He wanted to transcend the usual relationship between king and soldiers, and bond with his army as no one had before; I think he even wanted to build an unprecedented relationship with the Gods, though he never lost his awe of them. He wanted to transcend the limits of incarnate human life by making his name immortal, or by becoming divine.

He was in love with challenges, because to meet a challenge is to transcend our internal limits, of thinking, of fear, of strength. I think he lived on these thoughts -- "Is this possible? Only one way to find out... let's go!" -- and the inward freedom and joy they carry.

Urge

Even in his relationship with Hephaistion he was transcending the usual social mores, since they were about the same age, and the accepted form was between an older man and a youth. I think that passion arose out of Hephaistion's willingness and ability -- he had enough intelligence, wisdom and self-confidence -- to be Alexander's other half, which cannot have been an easy task. I think Alexander also had a passion for unifying people in a common goal, inspiring them to transcend self-interest.

If he had not been raised a warrior, I think he would have expressed that urge in whatever field he had entered, arts, philosophy, or what-have-you.

CHAPTER VIII

Alexander's 'pothos'

I wanted to understand what made Alexander break so many unwritten laws of the Greeks and adopt all those strange customs of the Asians, that amazed and upset his generals and soldiers. It seems that the Greek word "pothos" might be a clue in this matter.

Pothos means desire, longing for, regret, want. When you first look at this translation you may be surprised to find want, desire and regret all in the same word. But if you try to think about it, you will find this makes sense. Within most of us is a need to learn, to develop, to achieve our potential. It is this painful restlesness that pothos expresses.

Never satisfied...

Alexander was this kind of person; a restless spirit, never satisfied with what he had, always longing for more. He was thirsty for knowledge, amazed at the great spectacle of the world. His face shows passion and energy. He is impulsive and has the will to win. He wants to expand his horizons and live his life to the full. He has a very complex personality, a mixture of light and shadows, impulsivness and calm, selfisness and a great need to be loved, blamable vices and incredible virtues.

The Greeks hate disorder and everything that can't be rationally explained. Alexander is tempted by everything that is unknown, he likes the risk. Unlike the Greeks Alexander was highly imaginative.The Greek soul lacked those feelings that express the restlesness and the will to reach unbounded territories and explore new and unknown things.

Travels

The famous traveller of the Greek antiquity, Odysseus, travelled unwillingly and all he wanted was to return home. Reading the Odyssey we find the same word, pothos; the same desire (but not to descover new, unknown things); Odysseus just misses his home land. To have the whole world, even to have immortality is meaningless if you don't have a place to come to, if you don't belong somewhere. Odysseus's journey is a voyage of self discovery. To have a better knowledge of yourself is one of the most cherished ideas of the Greeks. It was even the most important point in Socrates' philosophy: "Know thyself". Knowledge was virtue, and only by knowing one's self, one can become a better person.

Both Odysseus and Alexander want to have a better knowledge: Alexander wants to know and conquer the world, Odysseus wants to return home, to himself. You may believe that they share the same feeling. And yet this is not very exact. Odysseus was away from home (he had been punished by the gods), he didn't travel willingly; while Alexander wanted to do this, he could not rest at home, he wanted more, he felt he deserved more. (And what Phillip once told him is very significant: "My son,look for yourself another kingdom, Macedonia is too small for you.")

Alexander had inside him that urge to win and was this together with a supreme self-confidence that led him to victory.

CHAPTER IX

Alexander Quotes

This article was co-written and researched by Lyla Sparks.

"When Alexander saw the breadth of his domain, he wept for there were no more worlds to conquer."

For some years now many posters on the Forum of pothos.org have enquired about the origin of this - perhaps most famous - quote about Alexander the Great.

A handful of websites attribute this quote to the English poet John Milton (1608-1674), but they never mention any specific citation or poem. An extensive text search to verify the attribution to Milton did not produce any results. Although Milton does make some references to Alexander in both Paradise Lost and Paradise Regained, it is never in the same context or in words matching the quote in question.

The origins of this alleged 'Milton' quote have been debated extensively on alt.quotations and on Quoteland.com. This has provided the following information.

- W.W. Tarn, in his Alexander The Great II, 262 (1948) says that it does not occur anywhere in ancient writings, not even in the Alexander romances.
- Burnam, in Dictionary of Misinformation (1975) cites Plutarch's passage as 'proof' that the story of Alexander's tears upon conquering the world is a myth. It might have been an apocryphal distortion of facts. We know that Alexander did weep on two ocassions (at least).
- Segrais, on this subject of a hero's shedding tears, observes that historians commend Alexander for weeping when he read the mighty actions of Achilles; and Julius Caesar is likewise prais'd, when, out of the same noble envy, he wept at the victories of Alexander. See Virgil (19 B.C.), in The Aeneid (translated by John Dryden).
- The reference to Caesar weeping after comparing himself with Alexander also appears in Plutarch as: "To which Caesar made answer seriously, 'For

my part, I had rather be the first man among these fellows, than the second man in Rome.' It is said that another time, when free from business in Spain, after reading some part of the history of Alexander, he sat a great while very thoughtful, and at last burst out into tears. His friends were surprised, and asked him the reason of it. 'Do you think,' said he, 'I have not just cause to weep, when I consider that Alexander at my age had conquered so many nations, and I have all this time done nothing that is memorable?'"

- Another text which mentions the quote is McGuffey's New Fourth Eclectic Reader, Lesson XXXVI (1866). "Alexander lived many hundred years ago. He was king of Macedon, one of the states of Greece. His life was spent in war. He first conquered the other Grecian states, and then Persia, and India, and other countries one by one, till the whole known world was conquered by him. It is said that he wept, because there were no more worlds for him to conquer. He died, at the age of thirty-three, from drinking too much wine. In consequence of his great success in war, he was called Alexander the Great."

- Robert Hayman, in Quodlibets Book II, 95 (1628). "Great Alexander wept, and made sad mone, because there was but one world to be wonne.

- Samuel Butler, in Hudibras part 1 (1663). "The whole world was not half so wide to Alexander, when he cried because he had but one to subdue, as was a paltry narrow tub to Diogenes."

CHAPTER X

Short Timeline

356 BC

July 20 - Birth of Alexander III, son of King Philip II and Olympias, at Pella, Macedonia (pothos of Alexander)

343 BC

Aristotle appointed as tutor to young Alexander

342 BC

Alexander gets Bucephalas, his personal horse (died in 326 BC after Hydaspes battle)

338 BC

August 2 - Battle of Chaeronea: King Philip's Macedonian army defeats Greeks, Alexander commands cavalry

336 BC

October [July] - Murder of King Philip; Alexander ascends throne of Macedonia (full discussion)

335 BC

May - Alexander crosses river Danube: establishment of northern frontiers
    September - Alexander ends revolt at Thebes

334 BC

May - Alexander crosses Hellespont into Persia

May/June - Battle of the Granicus: Alexander defeats Persian defense force

Autumn - Alexander captures Halicarnassus, Persian stronghold

333 BC

March - Alexander solves riddle of the 'Gordian Knot'

November - Battle of Issus: Alexander's victory over Persian King Darius III; Alexander captures Persian Royal family

332 BC

January-July [August] - Siege of Tyre

September-October - Siege of Gaza

November 14 - Alexander crowned Pharaoh in Memphis, Egypt

331 BC

Winter - Oracle of Siwa allegedly confirms divinity of Alexander

April 7 [Winter] - Foundation of Alexandria, Egypt

October 1 - Battle of Gaugamela (Arbela): final defeat of Persian King Darius III

October 21 - Alexander enters Babylon

330 BC

January - Alexander forces his way through Persian Gates: defeat of last Persian defence troops

May - Alexander burns Persepolis, ceremonial Persian capital

July - Persian King Darius III murdered by his kinsmen

October [Autumn] - Alleged conspiracy: execution of officers Philotas and his father Parmenion

329 BC

Spring - Alexander crosses Hindu Kush into Central Asia

May - Arrest of Bessus, usurper of Persian throne

Summer - Battle of the Iaxartes: Alexander defeats Scythians; Rebel leader Spitamenes annihilates Macedonian forces at Maracanda

328 BC

Spring/Summer/Autumn - Army split in five divisions against rebellions in Central Asia
Autumn - Defeat of rebel leader Spitamenes; Alexander kills officer Cleitus the Black during brawl

327 BC

Winter - Alleged conspiracy: execution of court historian Callisthenes
Spring - Alexander captures 'Sogdian Rock', rebel stronghold
Spring [August] - Marriage to Roxane, daughter of Bactrian noble Oxyartes
Summer - Invasion of India

326 BC

April - Alexander captures 'Rock of Aornus', Indian stronghold
May [July] - Battle of the Hydaspes: Alexander defeats King Porus
September - Army refuses further advance at river Hyphasis: Alexander orders retreat

325 BC

July - Alexander reaches Indian Ocean
August - Alexander starts march through Makran desert (Gedrosian desert)
September 20/21 - Fleet under command of Nearchos sets sail to Persian Gulf

324 BC

Spring - Alexander orders mass wedding in Susa, Persia: marriage to Statira, daughter of Darius III
July - Mutiny (or strike) of the army at Opis

October - Death of <u>Hephaestion</u>, Alexander's lifelong <u>friend and lover</u>, in Ecbatana

323 BC

April - Alexander returns in Babylon
June 10 - <u>Death</u> of Alexander after ten days of <u>severe illness</u>

321 BC

<u>Ptolemy</u> hi-jacks Alexander's sarcophagus and brings Alexander's body to Egypt (<u>Hellenism</u>)

CHAPTER XI

Detailed Timeline

359 BC

Death of Perdiccas III, King of Macedonia: Perdiccas leaves infant heir Amyntas; Philip II elected King of Macedonia

358 BC

Philip subdues Paeonians and Agrians

357 BC

Marriage of Philip II and Olympias, mother of Alexander
   Philip captures the cities of Amphipolis and Pydna

356 BC

July 20 - Birth of Alexander III at Pella, Macedon
   August - Philip captures city of Potidaea

355 BC

Birth of Cassander, son of Antipater, ruler of Macedonia after Alexander

354 BC

Philip captures city of Methone: Philip loses one eye

353 BC

Philip defeats Greek state of Phokis

352 BC

Persian noble Artabazus receives asylum at Philip's court

348 BC

Philip captures city of Olynthus (Chalcidice peninsula)

343 BC

Aristotle appointed as tutor of Alexander

342 BC

Philip's conquests in Thrace
    Alexander gets Bucephalas, his personal horse

340 BC

Alexander regent in Macedonia during campaign of Philip against Byzantium; Alexander defeats Thracian tribe
    Persia aids city of Perinthus against Philip
    Probable end of the tutorship of Aristotle

338 BC

August 2 - Battle of Chaeronea: King Philip defeats Greeks, Alexander commands cavalry
    Autumn - Establishment and first meeting of the Corinthian League: Philip confirmed as hegemon of Greece

337 BC

Spring - Second meeting of the Corinthian League: Philip reveals plans for invasion of Persia
    Marriage of Philip and Cleopatra; Alexander and Olympias leave for exile
    Autumn - Alexander returns from his exile in Illyria

336 BC

Spring - Officers Parmenion and Attalus take advance force into Persia

October [June] - Murder of King Philip; Alexander ascends throne of Macedonia

Autumn - Execution of Amyntas, son of Perdiccas III and heir to the throne; Execution of Cleopatra, widow of Philip, and her newborn son; Third meeting of Corinthian League at Corinth: Alexander confirmed as hegemon of Greece; Possible legendary meeting with philosopher Diogenes

Other events - King Darius III ascends the throne of Persia; Marriage of Alexander of Epirus and Cleopatra, sister of Alexander

335 BC

Spring - Campaign to the Danube; Battle of the Lyginus: Alexander defeats Triballians

May - Alexander crosses river Danube: establishment of northern frontiers

Summer - Attack on Pelium: Alexander defeats Illyrians

September - Alexander ends revolt at Thebes

Other events - Persian commander Memnon stops advance force of Parmenion and Attalus

334 BC

May - Alexander crosses Hellespont into Persia

May/June - Battle of the Granicus: Alexander defeats Persian defense force

Summer - Alexander captures Milete

Autumn - Alexander captures Halicarnassus, Persian stronghold; Alexander grants winter leave to newly wedded soldiers

Other events - Antigonus the One-Eyed appointed as satrap of Phrygia; Queen Ada re-instated as ruler of Caria

333 BC

Winter - Alleged conspiracy: arrest of Alexander of Lyncestis; Legendary miraculous passing of Mount Climax; Campaign against Pisidians

March - Alexander solves riddle of the 'Gordian Knot', Gordium

May - Alexander of Epirus invades Italy (defeated and killed around 331 BC)

May [July] - Alexander leaves Gordium

June/July [Spring] - Memnon dies of illness

Summer - King Darius III and Persian army leave Babylon

September [July] - Alexander falls ill at river Cydnus

September - Alexander arrives at Tarsus, Cilicia

September/October - King Darius III and Persian army arrive at Sochi, base camp near Mediterranean

November - Battle of Issus: Alexander defeats Persian King Darius III; Alexander captures Persian Royal family

Autumn - Parmenion captures Damascus: capture of Barsine, widow of Memnon and future mistress of Alexander and possibly mother of his first child, Heracles

Other events - Idarnes (or Hydarnes) re-captures Milete; Balacrus defeats Idarnes in 332 BC

332 BC

January-July [August] - Siege of Tyre

  Spring [Summer 331 BC] - Statira, wife of Darius III, dies in childbirth

  Summer - First peace offer of King Darius

  July 29 [August] - Fall of Tyre

  September-October - Siege of Gaza

  November 14 - Alexander crowned Pharaoh in Memphis, Egypt

331 BC

Winter - Oracle of Siwa allegedly confirms divinity of Alexander

  April 7 [Winter] - Foundation of Alexandria, Egypt

  Spring - Return to Phoenicia

  Summer - Second peace offer of King Darius

  September 20 - Army witnesses total eclipse of the moon in northern Mesopotamia: single 100% sure dating of the Alexander period

  October 1 - Battle of Gaugamela (Arbela): final defeat of Persian King Darius III

  October 21 - Alexander enters Babylon

November 25 - Alexander leaves Babylon
December 15 - Alexander enters Susa
December - Campaign against the Uxians

330 BC

January - Alexander forces his way through Persian Gates: defeat of last Persian defence troops

Winter/Spring - Five months stay in Persepolis, ceremonial Persian capital

April - Campaign against the Mardians

May [Summer/Autumn 331 BC] - Battle of Megalopolis: Alexander's Macedonian regent Antipater defeats King Agis III of Sparta

May - Alexander burns Persepolis

July - Persian King Darius III murdered by his kinsmen

Summer - Alexander dismisses allied troops

Autumn [Summer 329 BC] - Alleged but unlikely legendary meeting with the Queen of the Amazons

Autumn - Revolt of Satibarzanes, satrap of Aria; Satibarzanes killed by officer Erigiyus

October - Alleged conspiracy: execution of officers Philotas and his father Parmenion; Craterus becomes second in command; execution of Alexander of Lyncestis

329 BC

Spring - Alexander crosses Hindu Kush into Central Asia

May - Arrest of Bessus, usurper of Persian throne

Summer - Alleged massacre of the Branchidae; Founding of Alexandria-the-Furthest; Battle of the Iaxartes: Alexander defeats Scythians; Rebel leader Spitamenes annihilates Macedonian forces at Maracanda

328 BC

Spring - Submission of Pharasmenes, ruler of the Chorasmians

Spring/Summer/Autumn - Army split in five divisions against rebellions in Central Asia

Autumn - Defeat of rebel leader Spitamenes; Alexander kills officer Cleitus the Black during brawl

327 BC

Winter - Attempt to introduce 'proskynesis'; Alleged conspiracy: execution of court historian Callisthenes
Spring - Alexander captures 'Sogdian Rock', rebel stronghold; Surrender of rebel Chorienes; Defeat of rebels Catanes and Austanes
Spring [August] - Marriage to Roxane, daughter of Bactrian noble Oxyartes
Summer - Invasion of India

326 BC

Winter - Siege of Massaga: Massaga's Queen Cleophis allegedly concieves a son of Alexander (named Alexander)
April - Alexander captures 'Rock of Aornus', Indian stronghold
May [July] - Battle of the Hydaspes: Alexander defeats King Porus; Death of Bucephalas
September - Army refuses further advance at river Hyphasis; Alexander orders retreat
Autumn - Death of officer Coenus; Roxane's first child dies at birth at the river Acesines
November - Start of voyage down the Indus
December - Campaign against the Mallians: Alexander's lung pierced by an arrow

325 BC

June - Craterus leads part of the army through Arachosia towards Carmania
July - Alexander reaches Indian Ocean
August - Alexander starts march through Gedrosian desert
September 20/21 - Fleet under command of Nearchos sets sail for Persian Gulf
October/November - Alexander reaches Pura, capital of Gedrosia
December - Reunion of Alexander and Craterus in Carmania
Other events - Mercenary revolts in Bactria; Desertion of Harpalus

324 BC

Winter [December 325 BC]- First reunion between Alexander and Nearchos near Salmus, Carmania

Winter/Spring - 'Reign of Fear': Alexander punishes and executes Persian satraps who abused power in his absence

January - Restoration of tomb of Cyrus the Great

February - Alexander orders mass wedding at Susa, Persia: marriage to Statira, daughter of Darius III, and to Parysatis, daughter of Artaxerxes III

Spring - Second reunion between Alexander and Nearchos near mouth of the Tigris

April/May - Alexander founds last Alexandria (Charax) at the mouth of river Tigris

July - Mutiny (or strike) of the army at Opis, Mesopotamia

August 4 [September 3] - Alexander issues Exiles' Decree

Summer - Craterus leaves with veterans for Macedonia

October - Death of Hephaestion, Alexander's lifelong friend and lover, in Ecbatana

323 BC

Winter - Campaign against Cossaeans

April - Alexander returns in Babylon

May - Funeral of Hephaestion

June 10 - Alexander dies after ten days of illness

CHAPTER XII

Animals

Bucephalus was Alexander's horse (a.k.a. Boukefalas). Peritas was his dog (only mentioned by Plutarch).

The most commonly asked question on this site is "What was the name of Alexander the Great's horse". Find out all about the Great Beasts here.

Please select an article from the menu on the left.

The Legend of Bucephalus

Few horses have captured the imagination like Alexander's horse Bucephalus. Though not much is known about him, we do know he was a dark stallion, somewhat temperamental. Though he is described as black, it is likely he was the more common standard bay, which is usually described as "black". And though most people imagine a tall stallion, the truth is probably somewhat less grand.

Breeding Stock

The best breeding of Greek horse stock took place in Thessaly, where prime existing stock was often crossed with Scythian, Persian (Nisean) and Ferghana horses. Philip of Makedon (who built on-going cavalry developments enough to be considered by many to be responsible for developing the cavalry as an effective fighting unit) is said to have imported 20.000 Scythian mares to Makedon. His son, Alexander, claimed a tribute of 50.000 Persian horses, which continued the infusion of Scythian, Nisean, Jaf, Ferghana and possibly Caspian and other blood into the Makedonian horses. Since the Persian Arab is thought to have been introduced into Persia around 2000 BC, it is likely that this bloodline was included.

Few of these horses were tall by modern standards, averaging 13.2 - 14.2 hands, with the possible exception of the Ferghana crosses and some of the Iberian stock. We know that the Iberian horses mentioned by Homer were famed for their movement, size and spirit; the Nisean horses were known for speed and stamina, the Ferghana was noted for stamina, endurance and the ability to withstand hard conditions in desert lands. Along with imported stock, Philip had access to the native breeds such as the Pindos, Skyros, Pineias, Messara and Andravidas, horses known to be small but tough. Looking at the stock Philip used in breeding programs, one can easily imagine a hardy horse with stamina, endurance and longevity. It was from these bloodlines that Bucephalus may have been bred, in the fertile pastures of Thessaly.

Thessaly offered rich pasture lands, excellent for raising all types of grazers. Athenian archives reveal many brands indicating horse-rearing areas. Pherae horses carried an ax brand; Larissan horses were branded with a centaur. Pharsalus horses, noted for their quality since the days of Aristophanes (c.450-c.383), were branded with an ox head, or *boukephalus.* It is also claimed that the name Bucephalus was also ascribed to those horses with an unusual naturally occurring feature, a peculiar shaped white mark on their forehead (Kroll, 'Archive of the Athenian Cavalry', p.88).

Though no one knows the truth about Bucephalus' breeding or raising, Pseudo-Callisthenes presents a mythic variant of Bucephalus' origin. In this tale, Philip is presented with a colt bred on his own estates, the heroic attributes of the animal surpasses Pegasus. The mythic attributes of the animal are further reinforced by the Delphic Oracle, which tells Philip that the destined king of the world will be the one who rides Bucephalus, a horse with the mark of the ox's head on his haunch.

It is quite likely that Bucephalus was bred on one of the many farms that formed part of the Makedonian breeding program. His quality would have been obvious from the start. However, many of the breeds used in these programs were described as temperamental and would have represented a challenge to train, especially since training methods varied widely from the excellent to the poor.

As much as Alexander was bathed in legend, Bucephalus, too, took on mythic proportions. One can picture this lord among horses, with his held high, dock horizontal and his tail curved upward, his wavy mane floating up and down with every prancing gate, as the other horses gave ground, instinctively knowing this stallion was destined to be king of all domains. Makedonian royals were good judges of horseflesh. Overlooking the herd, Philip and Alexander couldn't help but notice the dark horse. Even the price of this animal was unusual: at either 13 talents (Plutarch) or 16 talents

(Pliny the Elder), the cost alone would have represented a great value, as the Attic weight to a talent was approximately 57 to 60 lbs of gold or silver.

Philip ordered his attendants to mount Bucephalus but as each and every attendant attempted to mount him, Bucephalus would spin, resist, and attack, especially when his back was to the sun. Eventually all those who attempted to mount Bucephalus had been thrown off. Horsemen know that most horses, left alone and un-worked for long periods of time, could appear to have become un-manageable. The average rider can be deceived into losing control, achieving nothing with the horse or themselves. But horses, equipped with a different but high level of intelligence, generally favor handlers with gentle common "horse sense". Bucephalus was no exception- coming from well-bred but intelligent stock, he would have need not only good training but a rider of equal intelligence and skill. It may be that Bucephalus had lacked proper training, it may be that he did not feel trust towards those trying to ride him (horses have an Instinct for knowing when a person can ride or not). But legend says the magnificent horse felt confused and afraid of his shadow. Maybe Philonicus was hoping for a cloudy day; if so, he didn't get it!

Philip could not see paying such a price for an unruly horse and ordered the horse taken away. According to legend, Alexander called out that it was a shame to waste such an animal because of poor riders. One can imagine that day:

Philip turned to look at his son. "Alexander, whatever do you mean?"

"I can tame this horse to ride," Alexander replied. "It only needs the right rider".

Philip scoffed "My attendants have been working with horses most of their lives, but you know better?" Alexander nodded, his mouth setting into stubborn lines.

"I know it would be shameful to throw away a good horse because people haven't been paying attention to the sort of animal he is." Alexander had realized that the stallion was nervous, unsure of his handlers, trusting no one but himself. He was also an animal filled with pride and a sense of self-awareness unusual for his kind. Pausing for just a moment, Alexander said with confidence " I know this horse and I'll make a wager for the price of the horse that I can ride him".

Philip reluctantly agreed, thinking that Alexander would be humbled and think more carefully of future bets. At the same time, he admired the fire in the boy and didn't want to quench it. He watched as Alexander slowly approached Bucephalus and carefully took the bridle below the chin. Alexander knew a frightened horse will jerk his head away and he wanted to be certain the animal could feel Alexander's own confidence. He gently stroked the center of Bucephalus' nose and lips with his finger Remembering a horse can kick a fly off its ears, Alexander calmly moved towards the stifle, placing his other hand on the horses body, rubbing and scratching the horse's flank, moving forward with his hand to slowly massage the neck top-line.

Horse Whispering

Alexander knew horses notice hand and head motions and respond quickly; he knew that because horses are not a verbal animal, words were unnecessary to gain a response from the horse. (In the future, modern parlance would call this form of training "horse whispering" or natural training). Alexander knew that horses, as a prey animal, often feared shadows so he led him by the reins in all directions, touching him gently, whispering comforting sounds, letting the horse see the movement of sun and shadow, learning there was nothing to fear in this strange field, surrounded by unknown strangers.

Slowly, Alexander eased onto the horses back. The animal stood, alert but calm, turning his ears back in an attempt to understand this confident boy on his back. Alexander worked the reins and leg pressure just enough to take his horse from a trot to a canter as everyone held their breath. He gave the horse more rein, allowing Bucephalus to move into a gallop. Keeping the horse's head up, he urged him with his heel and leg pressure into a full run After working the horse for a while in view of an ever-growing audience, Alexander stopped Bucephalus in front of Philip. A cheering crowd surrounded father, horse and son. With tears of laughter and joy, pride showing in his very gesture, Philip said "Alexander my son, Macedon is too small- You need to find another kingdom worthy of you!" And thus began the legend.

As one of his chargers, Alexander rode Bucephalus in many battles. The legend of Alexander's magnificent horse struck many an artists imagination, from the ancient world to the modern. Paintings of Labrum's Alexander subjects survive in the Louvre Museum. One in particular, The Passage of the Granicus, depicts the warhorse contesting the difficulties of the steep muddy river banks, biting and kicking all foes. Whether depicted as black, white, large or small, there is something about this horse that strikes a responsive chord in even the most jaded viewer.

Longevity was not the norm for the ancient chargers. Mortality rate was high due to extreme climate changes without time to adapt, severe hoof bruising from sharp rocks and bad splits without proper time to heal. Battle wounds and exhaustion were primary killers. But even in this, Bucephalus reached beyond other horses. Arrian states Bucephalus died sometime between the age of 28 to 30, a good age even by modern standards for pampered, well-tended horses. This would have placed Bucephalus a comparable age with Alexander when they first met. Some have questioned why Philonicus would bring a mid-age horse to Philip with a high price, but this discounts that many mid-age horses are preferred due to their proven ability to withstand hardship and the fact that their past experiences usually make them less likely to be flighty. It may also be that Bucephalus had proven himself a sire of quality horses and Philonicus may well have believed Philip would be willing to pay for an infusion of proven bloodlines.

Others debate that Bucephalus was of a younger age and died of severe battle wounds he received at the Battle of the River Hydaspes, 326 BCE. What is known, however, is that Alexander gave him a state funeral and founded a new city, Bucephala (now modern day Jhelum/Djemoul) in Bucephalus' honor.

Another charger that can be compared to Bucephalus was Comanche, the only survivor from the Battle of the little Big Horn, who survived his wounds and lived a long life. Comanche was owned by Capt. Myles Keough, this is the story of his last battle;

Comanche remained with his owner on Custer Hill. Evidence and oral tradition shows that all the other soldiers slaughtered their horses for cover except for Keogh who crouched between Comanche's legs fighting and holding onto his reins. When Keogh was killed, his one hand remained clutched to Comanche's reins. Shot with seven arrows, Comanche stood proud over his friend as the warriors were overwhelmed with sudden strong emotion that a man was so close to his horse as he held the reins even in death; because of the thought of bad medicine the warriors left the horse alone and the native Amercian women did not violate the body of Capt. Keogh. Comanche was nursed back to health and lived seventeen years after the Battle of the Little Bighorn as a pampered pet, traveling from post to post and loved by all, he was cherished and revered by the Seventh Cavalry and the entire nation as a symbol of survival in the face of defeat.It is said he developed a fondness for beer in his later years, After his death at the age of twenty nine, he was stuffed and kept on display at the University of Kansas, where he remains to this day.

Briefly, the horse used in the Oliver Stone Alexander movie was a Friesian. This breed developed in Friesland as a knight's horse but the breed was "lightened" for trotting races later on. They are still used as cart and carriage horses in Europe for the most part, though the lighter ones are also used in dressage. They are not as fast as some breeds (in the movie and trailers, if you watch closely, you will see many of the other riders reining their horses in so Alexander's horse can be at the front) but they are elegant and have a high-stepping vertical action, which can be easily felt when riding them. A Friesian was also used in the movie "Ladyhawke".

The Dutch registry does not allow (or at least has not) crossbreedings, and the Friesian has remained a "clean" line until recently. Sadly, the German registry began allowing outcrossings in America and there is beginning to be an over-abundance of high-priced crossbreeds there. I predict the American market will flood and in a few years, you will be able to buy them for less at the horse auctions. This is what happened to the Arab breed - and some fantastic bloodlines ended up going for meat in Europe.

In reality, this would not have been the horse of choice for the type of battles Alexander fought (also, they were not in existence in this form at the time).

Notes for Bucephalus; The Horse in the Ancient World by A. Hyland, p.149. Bucephalus' price- Plutarch, (13 talents) Pliny the Elder (16 talents). The story of the horse brought to Pella, Bucephalus died at the age of thirty, in 326 BCE. (Arrian.Ann, B.5.19, p.282;M.M. Morgan in X.Horse.,pp. 101ff; Plutarch, 'Alexander', in The Age of Alexander. Nine Greek Lives, tr. Ian Scott Kilvert (Penguin 1973 (1982), p. 257.6.

The Original Horse Whisperer's name was John Solomon Rarey. (1827-1866) His book was called; The complete Horse Tamer and Farrier, by Rarey and Knowlson.

Alexander and Lions

Alexander was a lion hunter. The lion subspecies that he hunted was the Asian lion, officially known as Panthera leo persica, which roamed free from northern Greece to India in Alexander's time. Our best evidence for Alexander's fondness of lion hunts is found in Plutarch (Alex. 40-41). After his victories over Darius, Alexander noticed that his companions were becoming acquired to luxurious habits. To ensure that they would keep focussed on war - even in the long lulls between battles - Alexander actively promoted lion hunting. He tried to set an example by exposing himself to the hardship and danger of lion hunts.

Lion Hunts

At least two separate occasions of lion hunts are attested in our sources: the Sidonian lion hunt (in Phoenicia, 332 BC) and the lion hunt in Basista (a.k.a. Bazaira, Sogdiana, in 328/327 BC). Both events indeed match with periods in which parts of the army must have been relatively inactive: the long siege of Tyre, in between the battles of Issus and Gaugamela, and at the advent of the Indian campaign after subjugation of Central Asia.

The Sidonian lion hunt is presumably represented in the well-known mosaic (found in Pella) showing Craterus and Alexander fighting a lion. The Sidonian hunt was originally commemorated by bronze sculptures made by Lysippus and Leochares (Plutarch Alex. 40; also Heckel, The Marshals of Alexander's Empire, 1992: p. 268-271). Alexander is said to have speared a great lion, so that an envoy from Sparta remarked the hunt had represented a battle between kings. Alexander's bodyguard Lysimachus also killed a lion of extraordinary size, but not before "his left shoulder had been lacerated right down to the bone" (Curtius, 4.14-17).

In Basista, a large enclosed Persian game reserve, another unusually great lion charged Alexander. Lysimachus rushed forward to help his king out, but Alexander pushed his bodyguard aside, stating that he was quite capable of single-handedly killing the beast. Alexander subtly reminded Lysimachus of his Sidonian adventure - such a wicked sense of humor (Curtius, 4.16). Alexander then killed the animal in one stroke.

Lysimachus' Lion Cage

These events gave rise to the popular story that Alexander had deliberately exposed Lysimachus to a lion. In Plutarch's Life of Demetrius Lysimachus exposes his scars to ambassadors "and told them of the battle he had fought with the beast when Alexander had shut him up in a cage with it" (Plutarch Demetr. 27). Curtius dismisses this "unsubstantiated" story as fake.

Heckel suggests Pompeius Trogus was the Roman advocate of this tale. Lysimachus tried to help Callisthenes, who was caged by Alexander, and for this attempt he was punished by being locked up with the lion. Lysimachus killed the beast by tearing out its tongue (Justin 15.3). In Roman times the story of the lion cage had become one of the three prime examples of Alexander's cruelty.

Asian Lion

The presence of the Asian Lion in Europe was attested by Herodotus and Aristotle. Herodotus recorded how Xerxes' Persian invasion army of 480 BC was attacked by lions while bivouaking on the eastern fringes of Greece and Macedonia. This happened during the night and the lions restricted their attack solely to Xerxes' pack-camels. Herodotus claims that the habitat of lions in Europe was small and was confined by the Nestus and Achelous rivers (Herodotus VII, 124-126).

It is generally assumed that around 80-100 AD the Asian lion had become extinct in Greece and in the rest of Europe. In Western-Asia they remained widespread for the time being. In the Holy Land lions disappeared during the Crusades. In Pakistan the Asian lion was exterminated in 1810, in Turkey in 1870. In Iraq the last lion died in 1918 and in Iran (Persia) the last Asian lion was spotted by railway workers in 1942.

Today the Asian lion remains only in Gir Forest, Gujarat, India. In 1900 the population of the Asian lion in Gir had dwindled to a meager 20 survivors. Thanks to protection the numbers in Gir have risen to today's standards of 202-290 animals. The Asian lion is slightly smaller than its well-known African cousin. A distinct feature is that the ears of Asian lions are always visible, while those of African male lions tend to be covered by the longer manes. (You can verify this by checking Alexander's lion mosaic.) Of African lions an approximate 30,000 still roam in the wild.

Another subspecies very closely related to the Asian lion - the Barbary lion or Panthera leo leo - became extinct in the wild in 1922 (in Morocco). This Barbary lion had been the dominant animal in the blood sports of the Roman arenas. Sulla had 100 lions killed during a festival in 90 BC. Pompey managed to have 400 lions butchered in 55 BC, as would Julius Caesar a few years later. Figures kept rising. Emperor Titus had a grand total of 5,000 animals killed during a single festival and Trajan surpassed all with 11,000 slaughtered animals during one event. Substantial numbers of these victims must have been lions. Some lions in Rabat zoo, Morocco, have recently been identified as Barbary lions (in 1974), though they are not 'flawless' specimens and a breeding programme has not yet produced very convincing results.

Royal Hunting

In March 2001 Martin Seyer published his dissertation on Royal hunting in Antiquity at the University of Vienna, Austria. Seyer emphasizes on the symbolic importance of lion hunts. As the lion "had been associated with monsters and demonical beings" the overcoming of these wild beasts confirmed the ability and the strength of the king to protect his subjects against enemies, rebellions and wars. The lion hunt became the ultimate allegory of legitimate power. Therefore, writes Seyer, not all representations of Alexander on a lion hunt need to refer to real events. Seyer: "Illustrations of this activity were an ideal instrument of propaganda within the frame of ideology."

In an aristocratic society a lion hunt was a political event. This was true for the Assyrian and Achaemenid kings, as well as for the Argead house of Macedonia. According to Seyer nearly each of Alexander's successors "stressed the fact that he took part in a successful hunt together with the king. [They] used the subject of the Royal hunt to represent themselves as a fellow-combatant of Alexander." It is apparently no coincidence that Curtius, in describing Lysimachus' intervention during the Basista hunt, immediately adds that Lysimachus "subsequently gained Royal power". This incident echoes an older story about the Persian satrap Megabyzus: "Megabyzus, who on a hunt had saved king Artaxerxes I from a charging lion, was exiled for killing an animal before his master" (see: www.san.beck.org/EC6-Assyria.html).

Hunting lions had always been a ceremonial Royal task. The Assyrian king Tiglath-pileser boasted that he had killed no less than 920 lions during his lifetime. For the Persian Achaemenids Royal hunting had become part of a long term planning process. Their big game was kept in large hunting reserves, like Basista, which until Alexander's arrival had been left untouched for four generations. But Alexander's lion killing record would not have come close to Tiglath-pileser's. Not by far.

CHAPTER XIII

Alexander in Art and Legend

1. The Gordian Knot

One of Two

When Alexander arrived in Gordium (west of modern Ankara, Turkey, March 333 BC) he found an interesting problem - the Gordian knot. The Gordian knot was tied by the legendary King Midas ('the Midas touch'). The huge and complicated knot held a chariot together and had no ends exposed.

Alexander did one of two things: he pulled out one beam, thus exposing an end, or more probably hacked it with his sword. It was said later that the person who freed the knot would rule all Asia. (Personally, I think that was made up afterwards.)

Thus started another of Alexander's legends.

Debate - What really happened?

The issue what exactly happened at Gordium has inspired lively Forum debates in March and April 2003. Here is a brief synopsis of the discussion.

Tre wrote: "[The Gordian knot is an] interesting story with two different endings. What Alexander did gives an interesting perspective into the psychology of the King."

In a response, Susan thought: "I see Alexander cutting the Gordian knot as described - Alexander was nothing if not quick-thinking and versatile - he knew he had to achieve the result and just went a different way to achieve it. So - Alexander did it. [Others] casted it in a positive light and found or made up a few prophecies that matched."

Janet disgarees: "I am on the side he would not cheat, and thus slipped the knot down so that he could find the ends; thus, proving his mastery over the problem. Pulling the ends, he unraveled the knot."

Marcus is very sceptical about this: "Actually, what I'd *really* like to know is: where else is the legend of the Gordian Knot documented? At one point I thought it was mentioned in Herodotus, but it doesn't appear to be. As for Alexander solving the riddle... I reckon he slashed through it with his sword. Alexander, demonstrating his no nonsense approach and impetuosity, thought [any more subtle solution] was too namby pamby... "

Maceik agrees: "We really don't know how he did it, but slashing the knot by his sword is really Alexander's way of doing things."

Debate - What do the sources say?

Karl takes the discussion to a higher level, bringing in the bias of our sources: "I prefer the namby pamby removal of the pin solution since this is the story Aristoboulos tells [us]. He was probably there and as an engineer would be interested in such a problem. The sword-slashing one seems more like propaganda, either from Ptolemy - Alexander held Asia by right of his sword, just as the Successors' kingdoms are called 'spear-won land' - or from an anti-Alexander tradition which represents him as a simple thug whose answer to any problem is the sword."

Marcus is not happy: "But we must also remember that Aristoboulos is known to have been an apologist for Alexander in his history. Therefore, he might have preferred to assign to Alexander a more 'intellectual' solution than what actually happened. Yes, Ptolemy might have been writing a propagandist version of events, but in a matter such as this it seems to be a bit too subtle for it to be a Ptolemaic construct... "

Tre thinks Marcus approach is too simple: "Alexander would not have cheated - [...] that would have invalidated the prediction. Things of that nature were considered quite grave [...]. Alexander certainly did not suffer from lack of grey matter, however, doubtless this little puzzle was probably rigged in such a way as to make sure the King won. I don't buy the theory that everything Aristoboulos said was 'apologist.' A careful reading of the pieces of his history embedded in Arrian shows quite the opposite [...]. Aristoboulos [...] does not have a personal reputation to protect, i.e. he was not involved in the major decisions, not being one of the principle friends [...]. It appears to me he was trying to defend Alexander from what he felt were the unjust accusations of others. Considering the times in which he wrote which were extremely hostile to Alexander, this is hardly a great leap of historical study [...]."

2. The Legends Surrounding Alexander's Birth

Around 1285 AD the Flemish monk Jacob van Maerlant composed his 'Spiegel Historiael' - 'A Reflection on History'. Fragments of the work were published in a modern edition by Amsterdam University Press in 1994. Here is a brief synopsis of the birth of Alexander according to the Medieval tradition.

Seduction of Olympias

The Egyptian Pharaoh Nectanebo [Neptanabus] is a skilled souceror who defends his empire by the use of black magic. Whenever enemies approach, he retreats in his quarters and casts spells to sink their ships and destroy their troops. When the Persian king Ochus marches towards Egypt with a massive force, Nectanebo receives a warning from his gods that this time his magic arts are likely to fail. Nectanebo flees to Macedonia where he meets with Olympias while King Philip is on campaign.
Olympias is impressed by Nectanebo's knowledge of astrology. The Pharaoh predicts Olympias will soon conceive a child from a god: the god Ammon of Lybia. The cunning Nectanebo changes himself into a dragon and has intercourse with Olympias, who firmly believes she is making love to the god.
Afterwards Nectanebo manifests himself in a dream of Philip. Philip tells his soothsayers he dreamt a beautiful horned god with wild hair was making love to his wife. His soothsayers answer that his description matches the Lybian god Ammon. Philip returns home and tells Olympias he knows she conceived from a god. But in his heart he has no peace with it.

Birth of Alexander

During a party at the Macedonian court Nectanebo enters in the shape of a dragon, then transforms himself into an eagle and escapes. Philip remarks that if the dragon represents Ammon, the eagle must represent Jupiter (Zeus). His doubts have now vanished. Immediately after this incident a chicken lays an egg in Philip's lap. The egg hatches and a tiny dragon appears, which crawls around the egg, then dies as it apparently tries to get back in.

The soothsayers explain this sign: Olympias' son will conquer the world but will die before he is able to return to Macedonia.

Nectanebo assists Olympias as she goes into labour. Alexander is born during a raging thunderstorm. The earth trembles and two eagles stand guard on the roof of the palace. Alexander has golden, curling hair like a lion. His face is cheerful and his eyes are bright and lively. His left eye is grey, the right one brown.

Death of Nectanebo

At the age of twelve Alexander is already fond of weaponry and he spends a lot of time marching with the army. He invites Nectanebo to come with him, as he wants the Pharaoh to teach him more about astrology.

In his roguishness Alexander pushes Nectanebo into a ditch. The Pharaoh breaks his neck. Alexander says: "If you were really good at astrology, you would have foreseen this."

Nectanebo answers: "Nobody can deter fate. It was my fate that I would be killed by my own son." Alexander questions the dying Pharaoh who reveals the story about the seduction of Olympias. Alexander buries Nectanebo with full honours. Olympias publicly admits she had been deceived.

3. The Legends Surrounding Alexander's Death

In 1977 a symposium was held in Groningen, The Netherlands, discussing various accounts of Alexander's death. The studies were published as "Alexander the Great in the Middle Ages". What follows here is a brief synopsis of the fantastic stories which circulated throughout Medieval Europe.

Byzantine Story

The Byzantine story about Alexander's death was written in 1388 AD. As Alexander returns to Babylon a woman gives birth to a partly dead, partly living infant. The human part is dead, but the living part has the shape of a monster. One of Alexander's soothsayers explains this sign: Alexander will die, his successors will rule. Alexander has the monster cremated.

Meanwhile in Macedonia Antipater has revolted and Olympias calls on Alexander for help. To prevent Alexander's intervention Antipater sends a poison, so strong that it has to be transported in a leaden box within an iron one. The poison is offered to Alexander by his personal cupbearer Iollas. Roxane nurses her dying husband.

After Alexander made his last will with the assistance of Perdiccas, Ptolemy and Lysimachus, mist covers the entire sky. A star falls down into the sea, pursued by an eagle. The statue of Zeus in Babylon is shattered to the ground. Thereupon the sunken star rises again, followed by the eagle. Alexander dies. His embalmed body is buried by Ptolemy in Alexandria.

(Study by W.J. Aerts)

Romanian Story

The Romanian story was probably composed around the year 1560 AD and closely resembles a Serbian version of the same era. Alexander returns to Persia and to Babylon and is reunited with Roxane. In his dream the prophet Jeremiah appears and warns him of his death. Alexander awakes in despair and is comforted by Ptolemy and Philotas.

Aristotle and Olympias arrive in Babylon. Then a priest from Jerusalem reports that the prophet Jeremiah has died; Alexander has Jeremiah buried in Alexandria. Alexander is poisoned by a son of Minerva, a wicked shrew from Macedonia.
The dying Alexander divides his empire in the presence of Ptolemy, Philotas, Roxane and Olympias. He foresees that Macedonia will be ruled by an Asian Empire in a distant future (the Ottoman Turks). He requests to be buried in Alexandria and states that there will never be a second Alexander. Then his horse Bucephalus comes to his deathbed and weeps for his master. Bucephalus kills Alexander's murderer by crushing him underfoot.
Alexander dies in Jerusalem. Woods and rivers and mountains weep. The grieving Roxane commits suicide by stabbing herself with Alexander's sword.

(Study by A.N. Cizek)

Spanish Story

The Spanish story was written around 1280 AD by Alfonso X of Castile. A woman gives birth to a monster half dead and half alive. A soothsayer explains this omen as the forboding of Alexander's death and the wars of his successors. Antipater plots Alexander's assassination and prepares a poison so powerful it has to be transported in an iron vessel. Antipater's son Cassander brings the poison to Babylon and delivers it to Iollas. After being poisoned Alexander tries to drown himself in the Euphrates but is saved by Roxane.

Alexander makes his last will. Babylon is hit by a violent thunderstorm and an earthquake at the same time. To complete the spectacle, there's a total eclipse of the sun. Alexander gives his last instructions about the embalming of his body and the construction of his tomb in Alexandria. Then he dies.

In a letter to Olympias Alexander had adviced her to arrange a banquet after his death. Olympias does so, but not one of the invited guests appears. Alexander is carried to Alexandria in a golden coffin.

(Study by W.L. Jonxis-Henkemans)

Middle English Story

This story was written in London around 1300 AD. Accompanied by Antioch and Ptolemy, Alexander marches to Babylon where he expects to find Darius' treasure. Alexander intends to make Babylon his capital city and raises taxes for a campaign in Africa. He recieves complaints from Macedonia about Antipater's rule and summons him to court. Antipater poisons Alexander.

On his deathbed the dying Alexander names nine heirs. Perdiccas gets Greece, Macedonia and Carthage. Ptolemy gets Egypt and Portugal. Philotas gets all the lands from the Caucasus mountains up to India. Antioch (a name common in the later Seleucid dynasty) gets Rome and northern Italy. The other five heirs are fictional characters with fictional names and they get various dominions between Italy, the Balkan, the Black Sea and Persia.

A bird tells the heirs the body must be buried in Alexandria, according to the will of the gods. After this is done, the heirs are occupied in wars amongst themselves. This is the way of the world: the head is fallen and the limbs are in distress.

(Study by G.H.V. Bunt)

Dutch Story

The book which may contain the weirdest story of all, was written around 1260 AD in Flandres by the monk Jacob van Maerlant. Alexander has announced this world is too small for him and he yearns for other worlds to conquer as well. In reaction to his attitude a plot to end his life is forged, not on Earth, but in Hell. The vile creatures of Hell brew a poison strong enough to end Alexander's life and they hand the substance to Antipater.

Meanwhile Alexander campaigns in the deserts of India with his ally King Porus and he reaches regions never visited before, not by men, nor by gods. There, two trees - the trees of the sun and the moon - whisper the message of his forthcoming death. Alexander bribes and threatens his soldiers not to spread the rumour.

Back in Babylon Alexander receives submissions from delegates of Gaul, Carthage, Germany, Spain, Italy, Sicily, the British Isles, Norway and Denmark. The presence of Porus at Alexander's side proves Alexander is a kind and forgiving ruler and submission is the best thing to do. It would have been wise for King Darius if he had done so too. Alexander adresses his troops and announces he now wants to conquer the world of the Antipodes. Next morning unsual natural phenomena occur: the day hesitates to begin. Alexander drinks poisoned wine. On his deathbed he tells his troops of an even more important task: four giants are planning to conquer heaven and enthrone his father Jupiter. So the gods have summoned him to come to his father's aid. Alexander hands his ring to Perdiccas and dies.

Now for a man who claimed the world was too small for him, a grave five feet long is enough. Alexander lays buried in an inconspicuous plot of land for a long time, until Ptolemy moves his body to a beautiful tomb in Alexandria.

(Study by K.A. de Graaf)

Epilogue

These Medieval stories are utter fiction. It is actually rather amazing that a few details appear to be quite right - like Ptolemy bringing the body to Egypt. What we have to rely on are the accounts of Arrian, Plutarch and Curtius (and Diodorus, Justin). All these sources agree Alexander died from illness. The illness manifested itself after a drinking party. There is no agreement that the illness occurred because of the drinking. All sources agree there were rumours Alexander died of poison. Arrian and Plutarch dismiss these rumours, Curtius says they were surpressed. All accounts agree there is only circumstancial evidence for poisoning.

Questions about Alexander often concern the truth behind myths and legends. Myths are still forming around his person. Recently a message in the 'Forum' suggested Alexander may have died from a bite of his pet monkey. That is even weirder than anything recorded here.

4. Alexander, Gog & Magog

Alexander & the Unclean Peoples

Some manuscripts of the Alexander Romance (Late Antiquity and Middle Ages) contain a passage about Alexander and the Unclean Peoples. It is highly unlikely that the original version of the Romance, believed to have been composed in Alexandria (Egypt) around 300 BC, already contained this remarkable episode. It is generally thought to be a Late Antiquity addition and it generally runs like this.

This short synopsis is based on a Dutch translation by Belgian scholar Patrick De Rynck of a fragment of the Late Antiquity Romance (published in Amsterdam, 2000, ISBN 9025346766). De Rynck argues that the origin of this fragment must me dated back to 500 AD.

Alexander reigned for nineteen years from Alexandria, then he defeated Darius, marched around the globe and ended up at the seacoast of Sunland. Sunland was where the Unclean Peoples lived: they sustained themselves by eating human foetusses, decaying corpses and still-born infants - as well as dogs, flies and cats. Alexander drove those Unclean Peoples to the north and he sealed the entrance to the north by building bronze gates between the two mountains commonly known as Ubera Aquilonis - 'Breasts of the North'. Alexander strengthened his gates with asiceton, some supernatural form of metal. He also forced the Unclean Peoples to abandon all uses of witchcraft, so that they would never be able to destroy the 'Gates of the North'. However, at the day of the apocalypse these Unclean Peoples - Gog and Magog being their foremost - will scale Alexander's barricade and will turn against the 'Israelites'.

Pseudo-Methodius

The content of this fragment was considered to have been part of the apocaliptic revelations of the Christian saint Methodius. Methodius was bishop of Patara in Lycia (south-west modern Turkey). He was born in 260 AD and he died a martyr's death under Roman emperor Maximian in 311 or 312 AD. However, most modern scholars tend towards the interpretation that the text was an invention by Pseudo-Methodius, who was a Christian bishop somewhere in Syria around 680 AD and whose real name is quite uncertain. The Muslim Koran however includes a passage very similar to this Pseudo-Methodius prophecy. The origins of the Koran can not be dated later than 632 AD, the very year that Mohammed the Prophet died. (This might even lead to the hypothesis that both the Koran text and the Pseudo-Methodius relied on a common source.)

In any case the legend of the Unclean Peoples became incorporated in the Alexander Romance from some religious origin during Late Antiquity or during the early Middle Ages. Gog and Magog - the most prominent names amongst the Unclean Peoples - are first mentioned in the Old Testament book of Ezechiel (38-39). Ezechiel wrote around 600 BC. In later texts the names of Gog and Magog appear to have been used ad lib to describe the various violent, hostile tribes from the north-eastern fringes of the known world: Scythians, Huns, even Mongols.

I have found that further exploration of this subject might lead one only towards questionable and unreliable sources from the darker vaults of history. In any case: Alexander the Great is always portrayed as the savior and protector of mankind who exiled the Unclean Peoples from the civilised world.

5. Alexander and Marco Polo

Around 1300 AD the famous Italian merchant Marco Polo, together with the romancer Rustichello, wrote an account of his extensive 20 year long voyages through Asia. During his travels Polo encountered, and later recorded, four legends about Alexander the Great. Of course they are romanticised. What is amazing is that the memory of Alexander was obviously still very much alive 1600 years after his death.

The Dry Tree

Marco Polo records the existance of the Dry Tree, or the Solitary Tree, somewhere in the wastelands of northern Persia. According to Polo it is the only single tree within hundreds of miles of desert (although he admits that in one direction there were other trees nearby). The legend has it that the Dry Tree marks the exact spot of the great battle between Alexander and Darius.

It's not clear wether this 'great battle' refers to Issus or Gaugamela, or both. The location - somewhere in Chorasan, near the border with present day Turkmenistan - is also impossible. When Alexander reached these regions Darius was already assassinated. Polo describes the Dry Tree as of great size, with green leaves on one side and white leaves on the other.

Please note: a solitary dry tree is also very prominent in the famous Issus-mosaic from Pompei, pinning down the precise location where Alexander and Darius came face to face.

(Though the story is fiction, solitary trees are not. There has been a similar famous tree in the West-African state of Niger, serving both as a landmark and a national monument, until it was run over by a truck driver in 1973.)

Alexander's heirs

Marco Polo claims Balkh, in modern Afghanistan, is the city where Alexander married the daughter of King Darius. He continues his account with the description of the nearby kingdom of Badakshan. The rulers of Badakshan, Polo writes, are the direct descendants of Alexander and his Persian bride. In honour of their forefather these kings all bear the title of Zulkarnein, the Muslim name for Alexander.

Balkh is the ancient city of Bactra Zariaspa, the capital of Bactria. In this area - in Nautaca, not Bactra - Alexander in 327 BC married Roxane, daughter of the Sogdian nobleman Oxyartes. Roxane had absolutely nothing to do with the household of King Darius. But in many tales she replaces Stateira, the actual daughter of Darius (married to Alexander in 324 BC; she bore him no children). Roxane and her infant son did not survive the power struggles after Alexander's death.

The last unicorns

Marco Polo fuels the popular legend that Bucephalus, the majestic horse Alexander possessed since age 14, was actually a unicorn. So not only the conqueror wore horns, his horse did too.

According to Polo in Badakshan there lived a breed of horses which were the direct offspring of Bucephalus and local mares. All of them were born with a horn on their forehead, says Polo. This breed was the exclusive property of one single member of the Badakshan royal family. He stubbornly refused to grant the king ownership of some of these remarkable horses and was therefore executed. In revenge his infuriated wife decided to destroy the entire breed. Thus the race of unicorns became extinct.

Alexander's barrier

Of Georgia - the region of the former Sovjet republic in the Caucasus mountains - Polo writes that this was the country where Alexander's progress was halted because the road was too narrow and dangerous. Alexander had, according to Polo, the sea on one side, steep mountains on the other and impenetrable forests in front of him.

In Georgia Alexander decided to build a barrier across a narrow pass between two mountains. Alexander built towers and a fortress and thus cut off the malignant northern hordes from the civilised world. Polo says the barbarian tribes were often refered to as Tartars, but their correct name should be Comenians. Polo uses the name Iron Gates for the pass which was closed by Alexander.

Polo's account is fiction. Alexander never even ventured in these regions. But the legend about this ancient version of the 'iron curtain' or 'Berlin wall' closely resembles the myths concerning remnants of a great wall found on the eastern shores of the Caspian Sea, attributed to Alexander (though this wall was erected centruries later). There's also a striking resemblance to the passage about Gog and Magog in the Holy Koran. All of these stories echo episodes in Alexander's career when, for example, he led his troops against the Scythian nomads.

(Polo mentions Gog and Magog elsewhere in his work and locates it in northern China. Classic Arab geographers even linked the Great Wall of China with the Alexander story in the Koran. Another possible candidate for 'Alexander's wall' lies near Derbent in the Russian area of Dagestan.)

6. The Seven Wonders of the Ancient World

Though the first list of the Seven Wonders of the Ancient World was compiled around the second century BC, it was destroyed in the great fire of the Alexandria Library, and the list as we know it today was written in the Middle Ages. Its origin, however, lies in the Hellenistic period after the conquests of Alexander the Great - all seven wonders fell within his new realm. Four of these wonders were in existence at the time of Alexander's reign and another was under construction, however, Alexander has a connection to all seven.

1. The Great Pyramids of Giza

Alexander did not linger for long in Egypt and there is no extant evidence of him having ever visited the pyramids. He may well have done so, and it was considered too trivial to record, or it may have been mentioned in earlier biographies and not repeated. According to legend, however, there is no doubt. Almost any article on the Great Pyramid at Giza will tell you that not only did Alexander visit, he spent time alone in the King's chamber! We have no way of knowing when or where this story originated, but it is more credible than most Alexander myths. Then, as now, the pyramids were admired. If the opportunity arose, it is likely that Alexander took the time to explore them. Even if he did not travel to Giza, it is interesting that although the Great Pyramid has fascinated and enthralled people for thousands of years, many obviously feel that a supposed visit by Alexander the Great adds even more to its mystique.

2. The Hanging Gardens of Babylon

Babylon was the city which Alexander probably intended to make his new capital of the Persian empire. He captured Babylon in 331 BC and returned there in 323 BC to meet his untimely death. Scholars today are still arguing over the exact location of the gardens, but they had to have been close to the river because of the need for a water supply. Alexander could not have spent any significant amount of time in Babylon and not visited the gardens, but was this the place where he lay dying, desperately trying to cool his fever? Shortly before his death, Arrian reports that Alexander was "taken from the mess to the river where he boarded a boat and crossed the river to the garden." A few days later, he was obviously in the garden again, and then "was taken from the garden to the palace" where he subsequently died. Could this mean Alexander spent the last few days of his life either in, or gazing upon, the famous Hanging Gardens of Babylon?

3. The Statue of Zeus at Olympia

There is no record of Alexander having seen the Statue of Zeus at Olympia, but during his youth he may well have attended an Olympic event even though he never competed in the games - he said he would only race if there were kings to run against him. However, the site had great religious significance and was also the location where his father, Philip II, began the building of the circular Philippeion after the battle of Chaeroneia in 338 BC. Philip's new temple contained statues by Leochares, including life-size figures of Philip and Alexander, and was completed by Alexander and used for the hero worship of the Macedonian dynasty. Anyone honoring the statue of Zeus in his temple had only to walk a very short distance in order to also gaze upon the figure of Alexander.

4. The Temple of Artemis at Ephesus

A previous Temple of Artemis at Ephesus burned down around the time Alexander was born, torched by a man named Herostratus who was seeking eternal fame. Legend has it that the reason Artemis did not protect her temple from destruction was because she was assisting in the delivery of Alexander. The rebuilding of what was to become the last great temple, and one of the Seven Wonders, was still in progress when Alexander arrived at Ephesus with his army in 334 BC. An anecdote tells that Alexander offered to pay for the new construction if the Ephesians would credit him as the builder. His offer was tactfully rejected; he was told that it was inappropriate for a god to build a temple for another god. Building continued without Alexander's financial support, and the temple was eventually completed some time after Alexander's death.

5. The Mausoleum at Halicarnassus

Alexander besieged and conquered the city of Halicarnassus where the mausoleum stood, completed during his early childhood. There is no question that he would have inspected it in detail - it must have been awe inspiring, even to Alexander. It was the first building of its kind, decorated with images from Greek mythology, but not actually dedicated to the gods. The Greek artist, Scopas, who also supervised the rebuilding of the Temple to Artemis, was one sculptor who worked on the building of the mausoleum, alongside Leochares, Timotheus, and Bryaxis, plus hundreds of talented craftsmen. Because of the similarities in design, some scholars believe it was the inspiration for the many-tiered funeral pyre or monument to Hephaistion, as described by Diodorus.

6. The Colossus of Rhodes

Though constructed several decades after his death, there is strong reason to believe that the Colossus of Rhodes was, in fact, a statue of Alexander. The Alexander Romance tells a remarkable tale of Alexander writing on his deathbed to the Rhodians and telling them that they were "the fitting custodians of my achievements; there is the second reason, too, that I love your city." This probably derives from the Ptolemaic period when the Rhodians had enjoyed a prosperous relationship with Egypt under Ptolemy I, a staunch admirer of Alexander. In 307 BC, the city refused to join Antigonus in a war against Ptolemy, bringing about the famous siege of Rhodes in 305 BC. The siege failed, terms were agreed, and the siege machinery was appropriated and sold to raise money for the creation of the Colossus, designed and built by Chares, a student of Lysippus, Alexander's official sculptor. Lysippus had created previous representations of Alexander as a god, along with a famous sculpture for the Rhodians of the sun god, Helios, driving his sun chariot. Chares' Colossus was also a portrayal of Helios, and ancient silver coins from Rhodes showing the head of Helios bear a striking resemblance to the image of Alexander on his own coins - leonine hair pushed back from the forehead, strong nose and jaw, wide eyes, and full cheeks and lips. Other ancient sculptural examples of Alexander as Helios have been found in Egypt, Athens and other places, suggesting it was fairly common to portray Alexander in this manner. The most famous Helios of all, standing guard over the entrance to the harbor at Rhodes, may well have been Alexander the Great, protecting what became known in the Romance as "his" city.

7. The Pharos of Alexandria

The Pharos or lighthouse at Alexandria would never have existed but for Alexander, who founded and designed the city. The first of many cities that were to bear his name, Alexandria stood on the Northwest coast of the Egyptian delta, a site chosen by Alexander personally. It was here that Ptolemy I finally brought Alexander's body for burial, and probably Ptolemy's son who began the construction of the lighthouse. Lighting the way into the harbor, the Pharos guided visitors from many lands into Alexandria, where, for centuries, they could still gaze upon Alexander's tomb.

CHAPTER XIV

Great Battles & Campaigns

1. About Alexander's Army

"Alexander inherited from his father the most perfectly organized, trained, and equipped army of ancient times."
J.F.C. Fuller, 'The Generalship of Alexander the Great'

Many books have been written about Alexander's army. This paragraph serves as a brief introduction to the subject.

Macedonian Army

Historical Background

Until the 5th century BC, before Alexander's time, Greek warfare had been a matter of amateur civilian armies on summer campaigns. Summer was the traditional season for war as it presented the opportunity to destroy the enemy's crops and grazing herds. Battles were fought by hoplites, heavily armed footmen lined up in phalanxes - opposing rows, four to eight men deep. Phalanxes would clash frontally until one side gave way. The hoplite carried a large shield, body armor, greaves, a short spear as a thrusting weapon, and a sword.

But in Alexander's 4th century BC warfare was becoming the business of specialist professional mercenaries. As Greece was a poor country, poverty drove men to the military. To hire oneself out as a soldier was just a good way to make a living. The Athenian mercenary general Iphicrates introduced light armed troops - peltasts - next to the phalanx. Peltasts were much faster than hoplites, more effective in rough terrain and they could harrass the enemy phalanx from the flanks or from the rear. The Theban general Epaminondas 'invented' battlefield tactics by concentrating his assault on one selected point of the enemy line.

King Philip II

Alexander's father, King Philip II, spent three years in Thebes from the age of fifteen (367-364 BC). This enabled him to study Epaminondas' Theban army. When Philip ascended to the throne of Macedonia in 359 BC he began to use his genius and experience to develop the brilliant Macedonian war machine. As Greek armies still consisted of both civilians and mercenaries, Philip should be credited for creating the world's first 100% professional army. In doing so, he combined the experience of the trained mercenary with the loyalty of the civilian.

While 'feudal' Asiatic armies were dominated by the mounted nobility and Greek 'democratic' armies by the infantry citizen, King Philip actually created two armies: the Royal Army of nobles and the Territorial Army of levies. This ensured a balance of power and contributed to the stability of the entire military organisation. Above that, Philip did away with seasonal campaigning once and for all. His force was a year round standing army, ready for battle in any season.

Royal Army - Companion Cavalry

Greek armies had used little or no cavalry. There was not one Greek horse at the battle of Marathon in 490 BC. When present, cavalry was used in dispersed formations for skirmishing or to pursue a routing enemy phalanx, but never as the prime weapon of assault. But the Macedonian kingdom traditionally possessed a strong nobility cavalry. What Philip did was to improve this existing Companion cavalry by drilling it to ride and attack in disciplined, dense formations for a concentrated punch. It was Philip who gave cavalry its prominent role on the battlefield.

The cavalry Companions were heavily armored horsemen armed with a thrusting spear and a sword. There were eight Companion units of 200-300 men each, one of which was the élite unit, the Royal Squadron or *agema*. Its task was to lead the advance on the battlefield and to protect the king when necessary. When Alexander crossed the Hellespont in 334 BC he took 1,800 Companion cavalry with him. They operated together with Alexander on the right wing during battles. Please note ancient cavalry rode without stirrups or saddles; these were not introduced before the 4th century AD.

Royal Army - Hypaspists

Without doubt the hypaspists are the most mysterious units of the Macedonian army. Historians still lack clues about what they exactly looked like and how they were armed. Adding to the controversy are the various names attached to them: Guards, Shield-Bearers and, after the invasion of India, Silver Shields (or *argyraspids*; their origin is equally disputed). What is certain is that the hypaspists were outstanding infantry troops who were capable of performing a wide range of tasks. During battles they served in close combat as an extension of the phalanx, protecting its right flank, and they were also well equipped for skirmishing, fast marches, storming walls and rapid advances supporting the cavalry.

Common sense indicates the hypaspists must have been, in one way or another, a flexible and mobile adaption of the original Greek hoplite. Philip had developed the hypaspists from his original body of Foot Guards. When Alexander crossed into Asia the hypaspists numbered 3,000 men divided in three divisions, one of which was the élite unit, the Royal Foot Guards or *agema*. This agema unit had the same role as its cavalry counterpart.

(Before the invasion of India Alexander is said to have added gold and silver to the armor of his troops; probably during this time the name Silver Shields came into being. It may have been that the hypaspists adopted this new name, or that the *argyraspids* were veteran units recruited from both hypaspist and phalanx battalions. What is practically for sure is that the Silver Shields were 3,000 seasoned warriors, boasting an undefeated record under Alexander. After Alexander's death they were hardly controllable: they betrayed their general Eumenes and killed their commander Antigenes by burning him alive. In the end they were dispatched to distant Arachosia where the local satrap had secret orders to wear them out.)

Territorial Army - Phalanx

King Philip transformed the original Greek phalanx into a devastating and awesome formation, the Macedonian phalanx. Because of their heavy shield, held by the left arm, the Greek hoplites had been restricted to using a relatively short spear in the right hand. Philip did away with the large shield and replaced it by a smaller shield slung over the left shoulder. This enabled the new phalanx to carry a long pike, the *sarisa*, now with both hands. The sarisa measured 13 up to 17 feet. Philip made the phalanx 16 rows deep; the sarisas of the first five rows were pointing forwards, producing an impregnatabe forest of armor piercing iron. The other rows lifted their sarisas at an angle upwards, forming an effective protection against missiles.

Alexander brought six phalanx battalions into Persia, each consisting of 1500 men and making a grand total of 9,000 Foot Companions, as the phalangists were called. The phalanx was well suited for a defensive role during battles - forming the center of the front and capable of stopping just any enemy attack. Because its effectiveness relied entirely on cohesion, an attacking or advancing phalanx could run into serious trouble, especially on rough or hilly ground. According to Arrian, at the battle of Issus the steep banks of the river prevented Alexander's attacking phalanx from keeping a regular and unbroken front, resulting in serious numbers of casualties. But the prime weapon of the advancing phalanx was the fear it inspired and the demoralizing effect it had on the enemy. In 168 BC the Roman commander Paullus admitted that at the sight of the Macedonian phalanx 'he was smitten at once with astonishment and terror'.

Auxiliary Troops

Heavy Cavalry - Thessalians

From Thessaly came the finest horses and horsemen of Greece and Alexander employed about 1,800 of them as allied heavy cavalry, organised in eight squadrons like the Companion cavalry. Although some sources claim the Thessalians were in fact superior to the Companions, because of political considerations they were stationed on the left wing to defend the flank of the phalanx. The Thessalian élite unit was the Pharsalus Squadron which acted as general Parmenion's personal bodyguard. The Thessalian cavalry was dismissed at Ecbatana in 330 BC although maybe up to 200 of them re-enlisted as volunteers.

Light Cavalry - Allies & Mercenaries

Accompanying Alexander's army during the invasion of Asia were approximately 1,600 light allied cavalry, hailing from Greece, Thrace and Paeonia. These units were equipped with javelins or thrusting spears and carried little or no body armor. Their main function was to protect the heavy cavalry and the phalanx from enemy attacks. In general these units lacked the exclusive discipline and training of the Thessalians and Companions. Most outstanding of the light cavalry were the 600 Thracian *prodromoi* or Scouts, used for reconnaissance and preliminary attacks. As Alexander was rather deficit in light cavalry during the campaign various mercenary cavalry units were added. After the campaigns in north-eastern

Persia units of Sacae, Dahae, Paropamisadae and Sogdians (and Bactrians) were included.

Skirmishers - Agrians & Archers

The 1,000 Agrians (Agrianes, Agrianians) came from the mountainous north of Philip's empire and were invaluable fast and versatile crack skirmisher troops - guerillas if you like - the Ghurka's of Antiquity. Whenever an assault had to be made uphill or through hostile terrain, the Agrians were there. Alexander used them during his attacks on the Pisidians, during the encirclement of the Persian Gates and the challenging sieges of the Sogdian and Indian Rocks. Agrians wore no body armour, perhaps not even a shield.

Alexander also employed 1,000 archers, half of them Macedonian, half of them from Crete. The Cretans had a reputation for being the best bowmen of their era.

Infantry - Hoplites & Peltasts

On crossing the Hellespont Alexander had up to 7,000 allied Greek infantry, consisting of traditional Greek hoplites. Alexander apparently made relatively little use of these troops other than as reserves behind the Macedonian phalanx or as garrisons in conquered cities. From the tribal areas of Philip's Macedonian empire came about 5,000 light infantry peltasts. The traditional Thracian peltast carried a bundle of javelins and a wicker shield. Added to these troops were 5,000 mercenaries, part hoplites and part peltasts. The initial number of mercenaries was relatively low, because Alexander was virtually bankrupt at the start of his campaign. Bosworth however estimates that at the end of his reign 60,000 mercenaries were occupied throughout the empire.

Siegecraft

King Philip had equipped his army with artillery and a siege train. The common artillery device was the *oxybeles*, a missile engine that could shoot deadly darts or bolts over a distance of a quarter of a mile. Alexander's battle with the Scythians at the Jaxartes river has the first recorded use of artillery in the field. The siege train included vital parts for siege ladders, battering-rams and siege towers, and many engines were built on the spot. Alexander's chief engineer was Diades who should be credited as 'the man who took Tyre'.

Persian Army

The armies of the Persian foe were made up of levies of numerous peoples, all dressed and armed according to their national custom. Thus, the Persian army can be seen as a celebration of the heterogenous harmony that - with only a few exceptions - had existed throughout the huge empire: indeed, a sort of 'United Nations peace keeping force' of Antiquity. Just as modern soldiers are willing to sacrifice their lives for abstract ideals - liberty, democracy, freedom - the original Persian soldier was also willing to die for a higher goal: his King. (Maybe one might compare this with the determination of the Japanese in World War II to fight and die for their Emperor.)

The nucleus of Darius' army were the Immortals or Apple-Bearers, the Persian élite counterpart of the Macedonian hypaspists. Traditionally they numbered 10,000 and Darius III fielded something in between 2,000 and 10,000 as his Royal Guards. Immortals carried a spear (with golden or silver apples at the butt), lavish tunics, a bow and a wicker shield. For their fighting skills the Persians hired Greek mercenary hoplites. Darius employed 10,000 of them at Issus, and these heavy infantry enemies were one of the main concerns of Alexander.

The remaining bulk of the forces were cavalry and light infantry from all corners of the empire. Prior to Issus and Gaugamela Curtius Rufus lists heavy Bactrian cavalry, Scythian mounted archers, excellent Hyrcanian cavalry, skilled Mardian archers, Barcanian horsemen armed with double-headed axes, Cossaean tribal levies, Cadusians, Cappadocians, Indians - and the list goes on and on, including "tribes unfamiliar even to their own allies". Persian cavalry was of remarkable standard; though probably not as well disciplined to attack in formation like the Companions, they outclassed Alexander's mercenary and allied horse.

At Gaugamela Darius used about 200 scythed chariots, equipped with sharp rotating spikes to demolish anything that came in their way. They were no challenge however for Alexander's mobile peltasts and Agrians. Heading the army were fifteen war elephants which could not make a lasting impression either.

Indian Army

At the battle of the Hydaspes King Porus' army, significantly smaller than its enemy, forced Alexander's Macedonians to fight their most difficult battle ever. Porus may have fielded up to 200 war elephants; they disrupted the Macedonian phalanx, claiming a toll of almost 75% in killed and wounded Foot Companions according to Diodorus.

The common Indian infantrist was the archer, armed with a huge bamboo bow as large as a man was tall. There seems to have been nothing wrong with Indian morale. Plutarch records that after some serious initial losses the Indians rallied and kept resisting the Macedonians with unsurpassable bravery. One hypothetical explanation might be that in the Hindu caste society one of the four castes were the Kshatriyas or 'Soldier Caste', which had its specific rules of conduct and behavior aimed at warfare.

Size

Arrian - as well as Herodotus - is notorious for recording Persian armies of impossible size. Arrian quotes a Persian army of 600,000 strong at Issus and over 1,000,000 strong at Gaugamela. However, the largest army of Alexander's time that we have reliable evidence of is that of Antigonos the One-Eyed in 306 BC, counting 80,000 infantry and 8,000 cavalry. Later Roman armies never exceeded this number: about 80,000 legionaries plus 6,000 cavalry were fighting Hannibal at Cannae in 216 BC and that was reportedly the largest army Rome ever fielded. So, the figure of 80,000 seems to be a sort of natural limit to the size of these ancient armies.

The size limit has to do with the simple need to find provisions. As Herodotus writes, the land itself was the biggest enemy of the traditionally huge Persian forces. Ancient armies did not possess trucks like modern armies do, nor could they be supplied from the air. No matter how ingenious their supply system was, they basically had to live off the land. Passing armies consumed the food supply of a country like a swarm of locusts. They could never retrace their steps: they would starve when returning by the same route. Prior to the battle of Issus King Darius left his base camp at Sochi where a battle could have been fought on favorable ground. Why? It is highly feasible that after one month's stay the Persians had no choice but to move on as they were simply running out of food and water.

Ancient commanders tried to keep their armies as small as possible. Though the Persians firmly believed there was safety in numbers, this basic rule would apply to them as well as to any other nation. Smaller armies were also capable of faster marches. The Macedonians did over forty miles a day during the pursuit of Darius in 330 BC. Armies as large as Arrian records - assuming they could survive at all - would have been incredibly slow. King Darius marched from Babylon to his base camp near in Issus within three months - a distance of 1200 kilometres or 750 miles at least. This he could never have achieved with his alleged 600,000 troops, especially as he marched during the heat of mid-summer and the supply of drinking water alone would have been a sheer impossible task.

Added to the armies were the camp followers. For Alexander's army their numbers are assumed to have been one servant or slave for every cavalry man and one for every ten infantry men. In India Alexander's entire entourage is said to have included 120,000 but his standing army at the Hydaspes is still estimated to have been approximately 40,000 strong - about the same number as he started out with in 334 BC.

Some probable army sizes

- Macedonian invasion force of 334 BC - 36,000
- Macedonians at Issus - 30,000
- Macedonians at Gaugamela - 47,000
- Macedonians at the Hydaspes - 41,000
- Persians at the Granicus - 25,000
- Persians at Issus - 100,000
- Persians at Gaugamela - 90,000
- Indians at the Hydaspes - 30,000

Battles

Fear and panic were the decisive factors in an ancient battle. Now, picture yourself as a simple peltast at the battle of the Granicus or at Issus. The frontlines during these engagements were over 2,500 yards long. You might be able to see what is happening in your direct surroundings, but of what is going on one mile down the front you can not have any clue. (If you had been at the dusty plain of Gaugamela, your area of vision would have been extremely limited.) In the mêlée there are virtually no means of communications - no radios or mobile phones. Even if your own unit is doing quite alright, this does not tell you anything about progress in general. Suddenly you spot some nearby troops running for their lives... What would you do?

Ancient battles were generally over within a couple of hours. In his *anabasis* Xenophon records how at the battle of Cunaxa in 401 BC the entire wing of the Persian army starts routing just at the sight of the advancing Greek phalanx. Not a single blow had been delivered and the armies were still some forty yards apart. This is not Greek propaganda only - it is a genuine account of what might have happened at many ancient battle fronts. Above that, the weapons of Alexander's time were not as deadly as modern fire arms. Arrows, stones from slings and javelins could hardly pierce through armor and they were rarely lethal. In an ancient battle armies suffered death tolls around 1% or 2% and the ratings of killed and wounded combined were around 12%. The ratio between killed and wounded was 1:10 or 1:12. In the modern battles of the last centuries the number of killed averages 5% and the total of killed and wounded up to 15%. The ratio between killed and wounded is something like 1:2 or 1:3.

In Alexander's time the majority of victims fell after the battle, not during the engagement. The defeated army would run in panic, being mercilessly pursued and butchered. Even on the victors' side many horses might die from exhaustion during the pursuit. (After Gaugamela Alexander's cavalry chased the Persians for seventy miles.) Another problem for the survivors of a defeated army was that their supply system fell completely apart, their provisions being plundered by the victorious enemy. Xenophon relates how after Cunaxa the 'defeated' Greeks had to butcher their own horses for food and scavenged the deserted battlefield for firewood for cooking - arrows, shields, broken chariots, anything that could burn. The lack of appropriate medical treatment hit the victors as well as the defeated; it is unknown how many of the wounded still died afterwards or would have been permanently unfit for further service.

When all this is taken into account some records of ancient authors appear to be quite acceptable. When Diodorus and Curtius Rufus claim that during and after Gaugamela 500 Macedonians were killed against 40,000 up to maybe 90,000 Persians, though this may seem unlikely it is actually rather probable. At Issus the figures of our ancient sources indicate that over 16%

of the Macedonians were killed or wounded. This is significantly higher than the average of 12%, suggesting that the Persians were certainly not the 'incompetent' army popular tradition wants us to believe. If Plutarch is correct in saying that the battle of the Hydaspes lasted for eight hours, this confirms the assumption that Macedonian morale was completely wrecked by this devastating, terrible 'Pyrrhic victory'.

Glossary

agema - élite units of the hetairoi and hypaspists

argyraspids - Silver Shields; Macedonian veteran crack infantry; 3,000 strong

basilike - *ile basilike*: the Royal Squadron or *agema* of the Companions

hetairoi - Macedonian Companion cavalry; heavily armored nobilty horsemen

hipparchy - four ilai of hetairoi

hoplite - heavily armored Greek footman

hoplon - large round shield of the Greek hoplites; wooden core covered with bronze

hypaspists - Macedonian crack infantry; 3,000 strong

ile (plural: **ilai**) - squadron of hetairoi; 200-300 horsemen

javelin - 4 feet or 5 feet long spear; missile weapon

pelta - wicker shield of the peltasts

peltast - lightly-armed infantry man armed with a bundle of javelins and a wicker shield; Thracian origin

pezhetairoi - Foot Companions of the Macedonian phalanx; infantry carrying the sarisa and a light shield

phalanx - Greece: battle line formation of hoplites, usually 4 to 8 deep; Macedonia: battle line formation of pezhetairoi, usually 16 deep and divided in taxis

prodromoi - Thracian light cavalry; mounted scouts armed with a sarisa

sarisa - 13 feet to 17 feet pike used by the Macedonian pezhetairoi (phalanx)

sarisophori - prodromoi

taxis - Macedonian phalanx battalion of 1,526 pezhetairoi

xyston - short thrusting spear or lance of the hetairoi and Thessalian cavalry

2. Major Battles

Many people wonder why Alexander is considered to have been such an outstanding army leader and why his battle tactics were so remarkable. This page is intended as a basic introduction to the subject; its aim is to inspire you to further reading.

Battle of the Granicus

- Date: probably May/June 334 B.C.
- Location: western Turkey, river Granicus (modern Biga, near Bandirma & Balikeshir)
- Macedonian army: probably 47,000
- Persian army: from 6,000 (Delbrück) or 15,000 (Fuller) up to 110,000 (Sekunda)

The Persian defence force facing Alexander after the Macedonians had crossed into Asia Minor was not a 'Royal' army lead by the Great King Darius himself. It was an assembly of forces under command of the satraps of the region. The Rhodian mercenary general Memnon was their foremost commander and the one who had actually advocated a 'scorched earth' strategy against Alexander's invasion rather than an open battle. However, his ideas were apparently dismissed by the Persian satraps who were hesitant to lay waste to their realms. According to most studies the main cause of Persian failure at the Granicus was the lack of consensus or a cohesive battle plan amongst Persian commanders.

Whether you accept Fuller's low estimate of 15,000 or Sekunda's grand total of 110,000, all studies agree that the Persian army at the Granicus was inferior to the invading Macedonians. The only real fighting strength of the Persians were about 10,000 cavalry and probably from 5,000 up to maybe 10,000 Greek mercenary hoplites. Whatever exceeded those numbers may have been hastily drawn levies from the region, with no ability to withstand Alexander's drilled forces. Delbrück even estimated the total Persian numbers as low as 6,000.

There is a nice little passage in Arrian who cites one of the first discussions between the king and his veteran general Parmenion. In all likelyhood it is part of a tradition to downplay Parmenion's role in

Alexander's victories and to justify his assassination years later. Parmenion observes that the Persian infantry is greatly outnumbered by the Macedonian infantry (!) and that therefore the Persians would probably withdraw during the night, making the crossing of the Granicus much easier. Alexander rejects this proposal to delay the attack, arguing that adjusting one's plans to the postition of the opponent would only boost the enemy's confidence.

So the battle started, possibly late in the afternoon. According to Fuller Alexander's battle plan was to send some auxiliary cavalry against the enemy flanks, giving the Persians the impression that the main assault would take place there. The Persians reacted in the way Alexander desired: they withdrew cavalry from the center (which was guarding the river) to strengthen the flanks. At that moment Alexander and his Companion cavalry rushed into the Persian center and made the decisive attack there.

Fuller states that we should not forget this still happened in the era of 'heroic warfare'. When the Persian commanders spotted Alexander's major move, they attacked the Macedonians with all bravery and courage you might desire from army leaders. They shared just one simple goal: kill Alexander. Often, they engaged in hand to hand combat in a desperate attempt to save the day. Fuller lists as many as eight Persian commanders fallen on the field, two committing suicide afterwards. Deprived of their commanders, the Persian army routed. It was not the number of eliminated armored forces that secured this victory for Alexander, but the number of their commanders dying a soldier's death.

Not that Alexander had been very save himself. He received a major headwound and was - indeed - almost killed, weren't it that his officer Cleitus the Black helped him out by cutting off the arm of an opponent. (While Cleitus saved Alexander's life at that specific moment, he was eventually murdered by his own king during their infamous brawl in Bactria, six years later.)

As most of the Persian cavalry escaped, Alexander encircled and butchered the Greek mercenaries. But the major impact of Alexander's victory at the Granicus was the loss of so many prominent Persians. His rapid advance through almost the whole of Asia Minor - up until the battle of Issus - was facilitated by the fact that there was hardly any Persian satrap alive anymore who could have organized some proper resistance against Alexander's progress.

Peter Green in his Alexander of Macedon presented a controversial theory that Granicus consisted in fact of two battles: one lost by Alexander - or indecisive at least - after which he retaliated and beat the Persians next day. According to Green this would explain why our sources have done very their best to conceal the truth behind blurred and contradictive accounts. Green is correct in his assumption that the written records of Granicus are too vague to allow for a reliable reconstruction of what happened.

Battle of Issus

- Date: probably November 333 B.C.
- Location: Hatay province of present day Turkey, just north of Iskenderun
- Macedonian army: 30,000 (Fuller, Delbrück) up to maybe 42,000 (Warry)
- Persian army: from 25,000 (Delbrück) or 108,000 (Warry) up to 600,000 (Arrian/Sekunda)

The site of Issus is now called Dörtyol, an unremarkable town in southern Turkey. Near this undistinguished place on the Mediterranean shore one of the most decisive and influential battles of human history was fought. And - to add only to its legend - it probably lasted less than one hour.

The first credits should go to the Persian Great King Darius. Whatever the forces under his command, and whatever his reputation as an army leader - he completely outsmarted Alexander prior to the battle. Darius had been assembling a massive force to counter the Macedonian invasion and he had moved this incredible number of men - even a low estimate of 108,000 is still a really huge army to feed, quenche and maintain on the road - from Babylon to the Mediterranean within three months. While Alexander was moving south along the coast, Darius took a clever detour and followed in Alexander's rear. We are told by our sources how the Persians feasted on massacring Macedonians unfit for service, who were left behind while Alexander's army had moved on.

Darius had for once intercepted Alexander's lines of supply and had disrupted the Macedonian logistic system. When Alexander realised his mistake, he immediately turned his army northwards. In fact he was trapped like a hunted animal. An unsuspectedly fast, forced, overnight march brought the Macedonians in contact with the Persian army. Darius had employed Cardaces (Kardakes) - young Persian soldiers - at his left flank. But as Alexander observed, they were assisted by archers. For Alexander this was a sign of weakness. If Darius would have had blind trust in his fresh Cardaces, the additional support would have been unnecessary.

While Parmenion lead the defence against the fierce Persian attack at the Macedonian left wing (along the sea shore) Alexander rushed his Companion cavalry towards those inexperienced Cardaces in the hills further inland. They could not stand up to the Macedonian assault. As they routed, they opened the way for Alexander to push his attack towards the center where King Darius was. Darius took to flight and the entire Persian army desintegrated. Game over.

But Alexander's victory did not come a moment too soon. Apart from the pressure on Parmenion's cavalry, the advance of the Macedonian phalanx through the center - against Darius' Greek mercenaries - was not going according to plan. The steep banks of the river Pinarus had disrupted the cohesion of the infantry, resulting in heavy losses to the Persian foe. Still, in the end this did not affect the final outcome of the confrontation.

Delbrück has an interesting analysis of Issus. Because Alexander's army was trapped, the Persians really did not need to score victory. A draw would be enough for Darius to isolate Alexander and force him to surrender. This observation - which was absolutely correct - determined Darius' entire battle plan. The Persians did not employ the full attacking ability of their cavalry but put their hopes on a successful defence. They were hesitant to pursue Parmenion's units, though Parmenion was overclassed and outnumbered - with disastrous results. Darius strategical decisions were sound, but he blundered tactically.

Issus is perhaps my favorite battle. The way Alexander turned great odds into an overwhelming victory is just beyond belief. The sheer contradiction between Darius having made preparations of assembling an epic army over many months, and Alexander totally annihilating his foe's efforts within a matter of minutes, just inspires your imagination.

Issus could arguably be called the most decisive moment of the campaign. After the battle the Persians had lost control over all territories west of the river Euphrates. That implied not only the loss of areas with a vital economic importance, but it also included the impossibility of ever launching a counter attack against Macedonia by sea. Alexander had executed the four basic principles of all military strategy: first organise your defences, then secure your supply lines, then capture your opponent's resources. Only after that, go for the final blow. At Gaugamela, two years later, the Persian Great King was already a beaten man.

The Macedonian victory at Issus was so fast that it enabled Alexander to capture the entire Persian Royal household: Queen Mother Sisygambis, Queen Stateira (Darius' wife) and Princess Stateira (his daughter) and Darius' other children.

Battle of Gaugamela

- Date: probably October 1ˢᵗ, 331 B.C.
- Location: Tel Gomel, close to modern Arbil (ancient Arbela), northern Iraq
- Macedonian army: approximately 47,000 (Warry)
- Persian army: some 52,000 (Delbrück) or 91,000 (Warry) up to 1 million (Arrian)

The respected lieutenant colonel Theodore Dodge was a great fan of Gaugamela (or Arbela): "Never were dispositions better taken to resist the attacks of the enemy at all points; never on the field were openings more quickly seized; never threatening disaster more skillfully retrieved than here." Although his statement was made over a century ago, it might still be valid today. Again there is a nice little episode in Arrian, in which Parmenion advices his king to try a night attack. Alexander rejects Parmenion's plan, claiming that he is Alexander and that Alexander simply does not 'steal' his victories.

From whatever side you look at it, Alexander must have had the intention not to steal his victory at Gaugamela. It could be argued that at Issus Darius had made the stupid mistake to employ his massive army on a narrow coastal plain, denying himself to take full advantage of his stunning superiority in numbers. But Gaugamela was fought on the wide plains of Asia - and Darius had had sufficient time to prepare 'his' battlefield. If the Macedonians would win here, they would have beaten the Persians on their own ground. For the first and the last time ever Alexander backed up his phalanxes with a second line of allied and mercenary heavy infantry, anticipating on the possibility that he could end up being entirely encircled by Persians. Michael Wood in his tv-series states, and perhaps rightly so, that Alexander in fact wanted this to happen. This should be the victory to end all victories: all circumstances should be in favor of the Persians so a Macedonian victory would remain undisputed forever.

Fearing that dreaded night attack, King Darius kept his army standing in battle formation all night, probably only adding to fatigue and demoralization. Alexander, we are told, had an excellent night's sleep, nearly overslept himself and had to be woken by Parmenion who had to remind his king that it was time for battle. Of course, this is probably a romatizised tale - but it fits perfectly to emphasize on the confidence Alexander had in this ultimate victory.

The battle progress of Gaugamela is far more complex than the earlier confrontations at Granicus and Issus. Parmenion, again, was ordered to take a stand against the Persian attack on the Macedonian left, lead by the capable satrap Mazeus commanding many elite cavalry units of the Persian empire. Alexander meanwhile advanced in an oblique order - some say 'diamond shaped' - against the Persian left.

Then, as the Bactrian satrap Bessus tries to encircle the Macedonian advanced attack forces on the Persian (left) wing, he leaves a weak spot in between the Persian left and the Persian center. Alexander and his Companion cavalry immediately take advantage of this opportunity. They fight their way towards the center where King Darius is.

Satrap Bessus was probably in the best position of all Persian commanders to observe the disaster in the heart of the Persian army. Though Bessus' Bactrians easily outclassed the opposing Macedonians at his wing, Bessus signalled the retreat so most of his Bactrian cavalry could leave the battlefield unharmed. But because Alexander had shifted his attack entirely to the right, a gap had also opened between the Macedonian center and the left flank guarded by Parmenion. And Parmenion's cavalry found itself under the ever increasing pressure of the bulk of Persian forces still willing to fight.

So some controversial elements remain. In the first place, Persian cavalry managed to brake through the Macedonian center. Instead of using this success to harrass the Macedonian front from the rear, the Persians were tempted - or ordered - to sack the Macedonian camp. If Alexander was aware of this danger (in the chaos of battle he might have been ignorant), he chose not to respond to it. Maybe he figured that a decisive victory in the end would compensate generously for anything lost now in the progress of fighting. As the battle turned heavily in favor of the Macedonians, these looting Persian troops were eventually eliminated by the Macedonian reserves which Alexander had deployed behind the phalanx. (There is this nice little tale of these Persians trying to help Persian Queen Mother Sisygambis to escape; but she refuses the offer due to her loyalty to Alexander.)

Secondly, there is this a weird account of Parmenion asking Alexander to help him out against the overwhelming Persian assault. Given the extent of the battle and the distance these messages presumably had to cover, this story is very unlikely. Allegedly, Alexander abandoned his pursuit of Darius to aid Parmenion - but this could easily be anti-Parmenion propaganda once again.

Third, but certainly not last, we do not really know what happened first: did Darius abandon his commanding position under the pressure of Alexander's Companions, causing most of his army to rout? Or did the troops - especially Bessus' cavalry - abandon their king as soon as they noticed that the Persian center was under attack? Accounts differ. Still, the outcome is the same.

In the end, the disastrous news of the collapse of Darius' center and the flight of Bessus reached Mazeus. Parmenion rallied his troops and started pushing back the Persians. By now, the battle was all but over. Alexander chased the fleeing Persians for thirty up to seventy miles before turning back to base camp. If anything, Gaugamela had proven the superiority of the Macedonian army and Alexander's generalship over the otherwise decisive courage of Persian leaders and their high quality cavalry.

The Persian Great King Darius had tried everything within his abilty. He had employed about 200 scythed chariots at Gaugamela, intended to cut down Macedonian infantry like life-size lawn mowers. His army had been accompanied by fiftheen Indian elephants, which strangely enough do not seem to have played any part in the fighting. The six thousand strong Bactrian contingents had included impressive catraphacted cavalry. Even the sceptical Delbrück admits that Alexander was outnumbered in cavalry by 12,000 against 7,000. If any battle has ever justified Alexander to be named 'the Great', this would be it.

Battle of the Hydaspes

- Date: probably May or July 326 B.C.
- Location: somewhere near the towns of Malakwal and Haranpur, nothern Punjab, Pakistan
- Macedonian army: 15,000 up to 25,000 (attack force) plus 11,000 (under Craterus in camp; Fuller)
- Indian army: 22,000 (Plutarch) or 34,000 (Arrian) plus 85 (Curtius) up to 200 (Arrian) elephants

It had been almost five years since Alexander's victorious forces had fought a pitched battle on the open field. They had been surpressing rebellions and guerilla warfare in Central Asia. They had made incredible attacks on mountain refuges and had laid sieges to reputedly impregnatable strongholds. But an Indian king, Poros, ruling over an empire in what is now northern Pakistan, was the single commander who had the courage to stand up against Alexander in the last of his four great battles.

Poros' army was much smaller than Alexander's. Though Alexander probably employed about some 36,000 troops on the actual battlefield, his entire entourage at these final phases of the campaign is said to have included close to 100,000 men. Poros did not rule 'India'. He ruled a relatively small and modest kingdom; so he could only levy little over 30,000 troops. But Poros played one big trump: 200 war elephants, one of the highest figures of these behemoths ever employed in any battle of Western classical history as far as we know of. Seleucos in 301 B.C. had 500 war elephants but - even as both figures might be exaggerated - Poros' number comes second best. Horses do not like elephants. Such a multitude of pachyderms rendered the Macedonian cavalry useless.

As Poros was guarding the Hydaspes river (modern Jhelum) with his elephant corps, he prohibited Alexander from making a crossing. For about two weeks - according to Robin Lane Fox - Alexander moved his troops up and down the western river bank. And Poros followed suit - until the Indian king became tired of all these false alarms. When Poros was finally 'lulled into sleep', Alexander left officer Craterus with a substantial body of troops in base camp. In secret the hard core of Macedonian forces crossed the river overnight. Craterus had complex instructions: Poros reaction to the Macedonian crossing would determine if Craterus had to cross the river too

- or to stay put. At least six different scenario's were discussed, according to Fuller. Summarized, Craterus should only cross the Hydaspes when there were no Indian elephants blocking his way.

When Poros found out about the Macedonian crossing, he sent a small force under command of his son (probaby also called Poros) to intercept Alexander's advance. Already too late. This Indian counter group was annihilated by the strong force of Macedonians who had made it across the Jhelum.

The battle proper opened with a sharp cavalry confrontation on the Macedonian right wing. Arrian says Alexander was determined not to attack the Indian center, because of the elephant herd amassed there. Poros' responded as Alexander had anticipated - by sending his right wing cavalry across the (still empty) battlefield to support the fighting at his left flank. But officer Coenus' and his cavalry had moved to the other side of the ranks, hidden behind the Macedonian infantry lines. Coenus was now able to intervene with the Indian crossfield cavalry move from behind the enemy's rear.

Whatever Alexander's battle plan was, Coenus' attack resulted in disorder in the Indian cavalry regiments. As they had to fall back, the Indian cavalry, infantry and elephant forces became mingled. Maybe this was Alexander's intention: to deny Poros the opportunity to use his forces as separate units. As soon as Alexander saw the Indian confusion, the Macedonian phalanx was ordered to advance. According to our sources everything seems to have ended up in complete mayhem. Wounded elephants do not retreat: they stampede. Friend and foe alike were trampled under rampaging elephants. (To add one more gruwesome detail: elephant riders - *mahouts* - carried a chisel and a hammer so they could split the skull of their animals when the beasts became uncontrolable.)

In all likelihood the Hydaspes battle was just utter carnage. No pretty battle. Plutarch suggests the fighting lasted for eight hours - exceptionally long for an ancient battle. Curtius Rufus mentions the use of axes and swords by the Macedonians to cut off the elephants' trunks. That Alexander was victorious in the end, was the result of his initial clever river crossing which had enabled him to take Poros by surprise. Even modern logistic experts admire the fact that the Macedonians were able to ship an entire fighting force across a swollen Indian monsoon river in just one single night.

In overview, Alexander had defeated a substantially weaker army at the cost of many lives. Arrian says that after crossing the Jhelum most

Macedonians entered the battle already exhausted and out of breath. Diodorus mentions 280 Macedonian cavalry and 700 infantry killed. When you apply normal battle statistics to these figures, this would imply up to 10,000 or 12,000 wounded on the Macedonian side. Plutarch states the Hydaspes confrontation "blunted" the courage of the Macedonians to advance further into India. In Curtius Rufus officer Coenus' claims that the Macedonians by now had lost most of their battle gear, armor and horses. "Will you expose this fine army naked to wild beasts?", he asks Alexander afterwards, trying to persuade his king to avoid a next confrontation with an Indian elephant corps.

Anyway, a few weeks after Hydaspes Alexander ordered the southbound retreat towards Babylon. Some controversial statements were made by (predominantly Indian) historians, hinting at the possibilty that Alexander was actually defeated by Poros. Poros' final statement after the battle - "Treat me like a king" - could be interpreted both ways around for sure. For some food for thought visit Alexander the ordinary, a webpage that advocates Alexander's defeat at the Jhelum.

Summary

If you would summarize Alexander's tactics displayed at the four main confrontations, three essential observations catch the eye. First, Alexander always managed to make his opponents respond in the way he desired. Second, he had an absolutely convincing talent for immediately determining the weak spots in the enemy line. And third, no matter how grim the situation, he never panicked, but always executed his plans in a coherent way.

Fuller observes that other commanders have equalled Alexander's talent to lead an army into battle. But the essence of Alexander's generalship was that he was also extremely succesfull in all other types of armed confrontations: sieges, anti-guerilla actions, ambushes. And it is this strange combination of mastery of all types of war that makes him unique.

3. The Hypaspists, an elite infantry regiment

The hypaspists were the elite infantry unit in the army of both Philip II and Alexander III. In translations of the ancient sources they are often referred to as the "guards".

When Alexander crossed to Asia in 334 BC he had with him three battalions of hypaspists, each of 1,000 men. Their overall commander was Nicanor, son of Parmenion. Nicanor died (of natural causes) in 330 BC; at some point after his death Alexander appointed as their new commander Seleucus, who later became satrap of Babylonia, and then king of much of the eastern empire.

There is some debate about the arms and armour that the hypaspists carried; however, as the campaign went on Alexander re-fitted most of his troops, and the hypaspists adapted well to the guerrilla warfare required in Bactria and Sogdia between 329 and 327 BC.

References

J.F.C. Fuller, The Generalship of Alexander the Great, London 1958 (Chapter 2 describes the units of the Macedonian army)

E.M. Anson, "Alexander's Hypaspists and the Origins of the Argyraspids", Historia 30, 1981, pp.117-120

E.M. Anson, "The Hypaspists: Macedonia's Professional Citizen-Soldiers", Historia 34, 1985, pp.246-248

R.D. Milns, "Philip II and the Hypaspists", Historia 16, 1967, pp.509-512

R.D. Milns, "The Hypaspists of Alexander III—Some Problems", Historia 20, 1971, pp.186-195

4. Alexander and the Makran Desert

Recently, in a TV documentary, it has again been suggested that Alexander chose the Makran desert route home as a punishment to his army who had mutinied in India by refusing to follow him any further East. Can this seriously be considered as a possibility? We question this view and give our chief reasons in this article.

There are two major considerations in this scenario:
First, the Makran desert itself, an inhospitable, pitiless landscape of rock, dust, sand and baking heat along the southern coast of Iran. The shoreline of today has advanced considerably leaving Alexander's coastline high and dry, a barren line still visible many miles inland from today's coast. Extensive geological and archaeological research of the region has been going on for over 50 years so there is considerable knowledge of the possible conditions there in Alexander's time.
Second, Alexander's nature. Although undeniably ruthless when the need

arose, he could also be unusually compassionate for his times, particularly to women and children. Is it likely that a man who was compassionate by nature (ie not from social pressures) deliberately led not only his men, but the wives and children travelling with them, into one of the worst deserts on Earth? Even if you discount compassion as an element in his character, you cannot discount his supreme abilities as a military commander. For such a man to choose, out of spite, to decimate fit troops who remained after sending the unfit home via an easier route would make no sense at all. They still had to get back to Persia through unconquered lands and have an army large enough to hold the new-won territories.

So what happened? Why did Alexander choose to lead his troops across the Makran desert? To protect and supply, or be supplied by, the fleet. Why the necessity of the fleet's voyage along this coast? One reason most often suggested was to open up a sea trade route to India. For that to happen, the coast would have to be charted, landing sites and wells would have to be mapped. (This route did indeed open up after Nearchos' voyage, because of the knowledge which had been gained.) But did he know how bad the Makran would be? Or did he think the route possible, having been deliberately misinformed?

Our main historical source for this incident are the journals of Nearchos (Arrian: Indica). This, we believe, may have been the original plan: That Nearchos, commanding the fleet whose assigned job it was to travel along the coast, would meet with the army at various points, and supply them with grain and provisions. The army's job, in return, was to provide wells and protection for the fleet whenever it put into shore to take on fresh water. In this way, the army and the fleet would return all the way to the Persian heartland and Susa. Or an alternative explanation for the Makran: the fleet may have been comprised of boats incapable of carrying sufficient supplies to sustain itself for such a long voyage. Therefore, Alexander had to protect and supply the fleet from the land in order for the fleet to survive.

Nearchos, a personal friend of Alexander's as well as being one of the chief officers, states that Alexander had full knowledge of the difficulty of the terrain over which they were to travel. He also gives another reason for Alexander's choice of this route: his strong desire to do better than Queen Semiramis and Kyros who had attempted to travel the same route with their respective armies, but had only managed to bring a mere handful through to the other side. While it is true that Alexander always rose to the challenge of outdoing the achievements of others, he was never reckless in his choice of challenges. It is, therefore, possible that Nearchos, who published his book after Alexander was dead, made this particular claim because Nearchos no longer enjoyed the protection of Alexander and had to survive in the hostile world of Alexander's Successors. He'd probably taken much blame- and continued taking it- for the disastrous march because of his failure to meet with the army as expected. Stating that Alexander planned to cross the Makran whether or not the fleet showed up was a way to take the heat off himself and pass it to Alexander who, safe with the Gods, was beyond harm. Alexander seemed to have a great deal of luck, but it was the kind of luck that accompanies meticulous planning and very detailed reconnaissance and local knowledge. So what went wrong in Makran? Maybe, for once, the local guides were reckless enough to give him false information, hoping the desert would conquer Alexander. (The people in this region were very hostile to invasion and fought fiercely whenever engaged.) Or it may have been the information was incorrect, supplied by those who thought their knowledge of the current desert conditions was sufficient- a not uncommon problem in some areas even today. Or maybe it was just a sequence of events in which Alexander's legendary luck failed for the first time...

The army had set out ahead of the fleet and the march to the coast proceeded as expected. The rendezvous point reached, the army waited for the fleet, but the fleet never came and no one knew why. (They later learned that the unexpected length of the monsoon and its prevailing winds had caused the fleet to delay putting to sea.) Meanwhile, the army had to be supplied from the land. It was a barren region and food supplies were soon exhausted. The replacement supplies which were to have sustained them were with the fleet. The land over which they had just travelled had been stripped by their march so they could not return that way, and without food, they could no longer remain where they were to wait for a fleet which might never come - for all they knew, it was destroyed by storm or treachery. Also without the supplies the fleet was carrying, they could not continue the planned march along the coast (even though they seem to have been able to dig wells along this coast and find fresh water). Therefore, the only choice left to Alexander was to order the army to swing inland instead and march through what turned out to be the worst of the Makran. One of the proofs that the soldiers themselves knew this was their only choice was the fact that they did not mutiny again, as in India, when the order was given.

Alternatively, if the fleet had to be supplied by the army and was dependent on the army digging wells and leaving provision dumps, then the army had to cross the Makran to reach the sea, no matter how bad the conditions were. Once they had completed their task, or as much of it as was possible, the same reasoning applies as to the route back into Persia.

So we contend the Makran march was not chosen for punishment or for glory, it was simply the army's only route home at this point and everyone knew it. (Alexander was an elected king; the army had elected him and expected to be kept informed of what was happening and why. A king who made bad decisions was very soon a dead king according to Macedonian tradition!)

Looking at some of the possible statistics concerning the incident gives another perspective on the march:

Plutarch says that Alexander had 120,000 infantry and 15,000 cavalry in India and yet only one quarter of this fighting force returned from India. In the context, it sounds as though he is stating that three-quarters of them died on the march through Makran. Yet this clearly cannot be the case, for Nearchos says Alexander had 120,000 total combatants when the voyage down the Hydaspes began. Subtracting the troops sent back with Krateros (the unfit veterans of the Companion Cavalry and other unfit troops, three battalions of the phalanx - commanded by Meleager, Antigenes, Attalus), the casualties sustained in India; adding those left behind to occupy and secure the land, plus those left with Leonnatos among the Oreitae, and minus the men who went with the fleet, we are left with an estimated number of 8-10 thousand (Tarn, considered to be too low an estimate) to 60-70 thousand (Strasburger) who entered the Makran.

(Arrian gives the names of various army units with Alexander but he gives no numbers, saying only that Alexander led the greater part of his army into this region and gives a detailed account of the sufferings of the army here.)

Going back to figures, if we accept (Plutarch) that three-quarters died, then one-quarter did not. This means that enough food and water had to have been found to have sustained the survivors through the worst of their march. If we accept Engels' minimum rations (ATG and the Logistics of the Macedonian Army) required for survival as 2 quarts of water per day for desert march and 1.5 lbs of grain or equivalent (we are told they ate the horses and pack animals), halve these minimal survival rations to starvation quantities, and go with Strasburger's higher estimate, we are looking at 18,000 survivors requiring over 4000 gallons of water per day, plus 18,000 eating the equivalent of .75 lbs of grain per day (though this is not considered sufficient to sustain human life) equaling 13,500 lbs of grain per day.

Looking at these figures, it might suggest that the Makran had a marchable route which was not quite so inhospitable during Alexander's time as research today seems to indicate. For those who believe Nearchos' story that Alexander had always intended to march through the Makran, maybe Alexander knew something that we do not which made it a more plausible idea. Had his initial plan worked out (ie to have the army be supplied by the fleet, or if the fleet had not been delayed), the disaster might not have happened at all. Alternatively, if the Makran was totally inhospitable territory, then for Alexander to have got even 18,000 through says a great deal for his leadership in a crisis.

5. The Pezhetairoi, the backbone of Alexander's army

The *pezhetairoi* were the battalions of the Macedonian *phalanx*. They first came to prominence during the reign of Philip II, particularly when they played such an important role in Philip's subjugation of Greece at the Battle of Chaeronea in 338 BC.

The pezhetairoi were armed with the *sarissa*, a long spear with a shaft made from flexible cornel wood, which had a much longer reach than the traditional hoplite spear. Because of its length the phalanx could present the spearpoints of around five files of men; which made the phalanx almost impenetrable, and fearsome to oppose.

Tactically, the pezhetairoi were best used as a strong defensive line, rather than as shock troops. The length of the sarissa, while making them an awesome enemy to oppose, severely limited their manoeuvrability, and if they were taken in flank or rear they had little chance of responding. This was particularly clear at the Battle of Gaugamela in 331 BC, when the rapid advance of the right wing caused a breach to open between two of the battalions of pezhetairoi—a force of enemy cavalry broke through and, had it not been for a lack of discipline in their own command, and for Alexander's placing of a second line of traditional hoplites in reserve, the phalanx might have been destroyed from the rear.

Apart from in pitched battles the pezhetairoi and their sarissas were not very practical; it is supposed that they were re-armed, and their tactics adapted, to suit the guerrilla warfare that was prevalent, and necessary, in Bactria and Sogdia.

Pezhetairoi Battalions

The battalions of pezhetairoi appear to have been organised on a regional basis, at least to begin with. We know of battalions named for the regions of **Orestis/Lyncestis** (two battalions probably combining men from both regions), **Elimaea** and **Tymphaea** - if all pezhetairoi were from Upper Macedonia then we would expect the other battalions to have represented **Eordaea** and **Pelagonia**.

In 334 BC Alexander took six battalions of pezhetairoi with him to Asia. By the time the army moved into India in 327 BC a seventh had been added.

- At the Battle of the Granicus the battalions were those of (from right to left): Perdiccas, Coenus, Amyntas, Philip, Meleager, and Craterus (Arr. 1.14.2).

- At the Battle of Issus the battalions were those of (from right to left): Coenus, Perdiccas, Craterus, Meleager, Ptolemy (replacing Philip), and Amyntas (Arr. 2.8.3-4).

- At the Battle of Gaugamela the battalions were those of (from right to left): Coenus, Perdiccas, Meleager, Polyperchon (replacing Ptolemy), Simmias (deputising for Amyntas, who was recruiting in Macedonia), and Craterus (Arr. 3.11.9-10).

- At the Battle of the Hydaspes only five battalions took part, and were those of (from right to left): Antigenes, Cleitus the White, Meleager, Attalus, and Gorgias. The other battalions (those of Polyperchon and Alcetas) remained on the western bank of the Hydaspes, under the command of Craterus, and crossed only when Alexander was victorious, in order to continue with the pursuit of the fleeing Indians. (There is much supposition and guesswork about this battle, however—see J.F.C. Fuller, 1957, pp.180-199.)

References

- J.F.C. Fuller, *The Generalship of Alexander the Great*, NJ, 1960
F.E. Adcock, *The Greek and Macedonian Art of War*, California, 1957
D. Lonsdale, Alexander, Killer of Men. *Alexander the Great and the Macedonian Art of War*, London, 2004

6. A brief summary of Alexander's battles in Asia

The excuse to invade Asia was to liberate the Greek cities taken by the "barbaric" Persians some years before. Alexander's motives must have been a little more ambitious. He crossed the Hellespont in 334 and is supposed to have symbolically thrown a spear into Asian soil as he led the way ashore in full armour.

He fought several pitched battles as he worked towards Babylon. On the way he stopped off at Troy and swiped the armour there which was supposedly from Homer's time.

Eventually he came head to head with King Darius at Issus on the north-east Mediterranean coast. Although Alexander was advancing south he was surprised to find Darius approaching from his North! The two armies had in fact been playing a rather advanced game of hide and seek. Alexander was not phased by the unexpected appearance and simply turned around his well drilled army. Alexander did get one shock which didn't exactly endear Darius to him. He had left hundreds of wounded behind near Issus in a hospital. Darius' army slaughtered them to a man. Not very sporting.

No-one really knows where the battle took place. However - it is almost certain that Alexander was outnumbered anywhere from 8:1 upwards. Even so, he held back a reserve force, apparently the first time this was ever done*. He then routed the Persians and Darius fled.

After the battle came two of Alexander's more famous quotes. The first was when he came upon Darius's tent in all its finery, with golden throne, bath, carpets etc. Alexander was known for living in spartan conditions by comparison and is said to have commented:

"So this is what it means to be a King."

The other famous event is one that gives us a big hint as to how close Alexander and Hephaestion were. Alexander not only captured Darius's throne tent, he also found himself with Darius's complete entourage. Darius hadn't done things by halves! He was somewhat confident in achieving victory and had brought with him:

Alexander hung on to all the women, and by all accounts treated them with great deference and honour "due to their station". The famous event is that when Alexander and Hephaestion went to meet Sisygambis, she prostrated herself at the feet of the most kingly figure she saw. Unfortunately she chose the taller Hephaestion! Alexander is said to have responded not with a dagger between the shoulder blades but with:

"Don't worry mother, he is Alexander too."

An interesting sideline to this is that later when Sisygambis had a chance to be returned to Persian hands, she refused to go. It is thought she and Alexander became very close.

*I remember 'Macedon' imagining Alexander's generals' reaction to this.

"We're outnumbered eight to one and you are going to keep thousands in reserve?!?!"

One interesting battle was at Tyre - where the Tyrians walled themselves in their island fortress. Alexander couldn't leave them to attack his rear and he could not attack by sea so he decided to build a land bridge. Apparently this bridge still exists - although I haven't seen it :-) Ironically he eventually took Tyre by sea in a very brutal battle - the Tyrians fired red hot sand at Alexander's advancing ships which was not considered very polite even then. All the Tyrians were slaughtered.

Darius finally met his end at the hands of his own people after the battle of Guagamela (Assyria). They tied him to a cart as a gift to win Alexander's favour. Then they stabbed him! I'm not sure why (any clues folks). Alexander only found Darius after he had died.

He then pushed on towards India via Afghanistan. One of his more brilliant acts was the capture of the Sogdian Rock. At the top of the said rock was Oxyartes, who felt safe because of the sheer cliffs on each side. He taunted Alexander to send up men with wings to capture the fortress. Alexander duly obliged. He sent up 300 experiences climbers during the night with the promise of fabulous wealth if they made it. The climb - a "very severe" in mountaineering parlance was completed by 90% of the soldiers. In the morning Oxyartes was appalled to see these men "with wings" waving down at him. He surrendered. Alexander and he then became good friends - Alexander married his sister Roxanne.

Alexander pushed on towards India and in another brilliant move defeated King Porus. Porus had 200 elephants, and was lined up on the opposite bank of the Hydapses which was beginning to rise. Alexander played an elaborate hoax on Porus. Every night he got a third of his army to pretend to cross the river and attack. This went on for weeks until one dark, rainy night Alexander did attack. He crossed the river way upstream and hit Porus' troops from two sides. They were of course in bed, having got bored of getting ready to fight every night. Strangely Alexander became good friends with Porus too. In the end Alexander's troops turned him back from India because they were homesick. In a terrible march across the desert in southern Iran he lost thousands of men to the heat and lack of water. Eventually he found his way back to Babylon, but was very badly injured by an arrow on the way. Throughout his campaigns he fought with a brilliance that was before his time. He also was a ruthless destroyer of those who opposed him and that should not be forgotten! Would you want your nose and lips sliced off?

- 3000 talents of gold (around £2,000,000,000 today - one talent was 27kg of metal (60 lbs) - the amount of weight that a man could carry all day).
- Darius's mother, Sisygambis.
- Darius's wife, Stateira.
- Several other princesses and noblewomen.

7. A brief summary of Alexander's Progress through Greece

Philip was not loved by the Athenians. They saw him as a threat because he was empire building in Macedon. They also thought that he was a bit of a barbarian. Ultimately he was forced into pitched battle with them. With Alexander as an able partner he beat the Athenians in a pitched battle and took total control of mainland Greece. It was a crushing victory, with the famous "Sacred Band", which had never retreated, being killed to the last man. Alexander was 17. Alexander must have learned a lot on the march south to the final battle plain at Chaeronea. Thebes, which had betrayed a treaty and gone over to the Athenian side was besieged and totally destroyed. 6,000 were killed, and the remaining 30,000 were sold into slavery. The finality and brutality of the conquest was something that crops up throughout Alexander's conquests. His basic tenet (I think) was this:
"If you go along with my rule you will be rewarded with your lives, my protection and my taxes. If you go against me I will conquer you. If you betray me you will be utterly (and nastily) destroyed."
Maybe he would have put it slightly better.
Anyway, Alexander was sent to Athens to offer terms. He was welcomed with great enthusiasm (well, they were hardly going to boo someone who had just slaughtered the defence force for the city were they.....).

CHAPTER XV

Death

1. Burial

Alexander was taken ill in Babylon, and died a few days later. His last few days are carefully documented. It took some days before he was finally declared dead and no one really knows what he died of. Was it poison, or just the endless campaigns catching up with him? If we found his body, which was mummified and hung around in Alexandria for a good 300 years, we might get a better idea. The tomb disappeared a long time ago.

Various people stole his burial gifts, including his nose, cloak, ring, breastplate and shield. The thieves were people like Augustus and Caligula. Even the solid gold sarcophagus got melted down for coinage and replaced with one of glass. The tomb disappeared some time in the 4th century A.D.?

In February 1995 the Greek archaeologist Liana Souvaltzis claimed to have found Alexander's tomb. Her 'new' tomb was located in the Siwa Oasis, Egypt, and not in Alexandria, where it had been visited many times in Antiquity. Should that surprise us? After all he was regarded as a God in many quarters. Perhaps his body was taken to Siwa to save it from the ravages of the dark ages. Anyway, Souvaltzis' discovery proved to be a hoax. So the location of the tomb remains a mystery. Will we ever know?

2. Alexander's death

In June 323 BC Babylon was living one last glorious moment of its history. Young and full of life, Alexander came back to the capital of his empire after he had got to the end of the known world. He was 32; he walked many miles since he had left Pella wanting to fulfill dreams that seemed impossible to all but him. Believing in himself and in his fate, he led his men to victory against the greatest military force of his time, the Persian Empire.

In Babylon Alexander's disease started suddenly (during a drinking party). The king was making preparations for new adventures and conquests. Although he was feeling weaker and weaker he was determined to start his new expedition. The army would leave, to be followed by the fleet one day later. But Alexander was not strong enough to fight the fever. He summoned his officers to direct that they see all was in order for the expedition; but the expedition was already one day delayed without the king realising it. A few days after this he was too weak to converse and direct his officers. Then the troops, aware from the delay that something was seriously wrong with the king, entered the palace to see him. He was only able to raise his eyes in greeting as they passed by, in their grief as speechless as he. The next day Alexander died.

Modern physicians still argue about the cause of his death. What has been written by ancient historians on Alexander's death seems to be not enough to establish a certain diagnosis. It could have been malaria, pneumonia or even poison that killed him.

3. Death of Philip: Murder or Assassination?

Murder: *the unlawful and malicious or premeditated killing of one human being by another.*

Assassination: *the killing of a politically important person (the underlying motive being to bring about some political change).*

This is an examination into the death of Philip, Alexander's father. It is an article of speculation based on our interpretation of the data. We wish to point out that the currently available ancient and modern sources exhibit some degree of confusion regarding the facts leading up to the day of the event, the facts regarding the murder/assassination itself, and the subsequent events that followed. We have attempted to examine the evidence and cite possible scenarios.

The major characters include:

Philip, King of Macedon

Olympias, wife to Philip and mother to Alexander III and Cleopatra

Alexander III, son of Philip and Olympias

Alexander, King of Molossia, brother to Olympias, marries Cleopatra, Philip's daughter

Cleopatra, sister to Alexander III, daughter of Olympias and Philip

Cleopatra -E, niece of Attalus (some sources list Attalus as her father), Philip's young wife

Attalus - some confusion remains regarding Attalus. In the sources, he is listed variously as Cleopatra-E's father, brother, guardian, or uncle. However, because some sources indicate General Attalus was in Asia Minor at the time of Philip's death, and for reasons to follow, we have decided to assume there were two men named Attalus, who may or may not have been related: General Attalus, Cleopatra-E's uncle and guardian, and **Attalos**, a Bodyguard (We have changed the spelling of the names for ease of reading.)

Parmenion, a General, related to General Attalus by marriage ties

Leonnatus and **Perdiccas**, Bodyguards, from collateral Macedonian royal branches

Heromenes, Alexander and **Arrhabaeus**, sons of Aeropus, another collateral royal branch

Pausanius-1, who killed Philip

Pausanius-2, who committed suicide, of sorts, to prove his valour

Note: There were traditionally seven Bodyguards (Somatophylakes) assigned to the King. The use of caps indicates these in this article. These men were traditionally sons of aristo houses, usually in their 20's-early 30's and at the peak of fitness and training. This high position served two purposes: to give protection to the King and to hold the families hostage to obedience while giving them honour at the same time.

Here are the facts we began with:

In ancient sources(1) a charge was laid against Alexander that he incited Pausanias-1 to murder his father, King Philip. There is no doubt in those sources that it was Pausanius-1, a member of the King's Bodyguard, who actually plunged the instrument of death into Philip's chest. But what was his motive? Was it purely personal as attested by Aristotle, and therefore murder, or was it from some political motive (with or without accomplices) as recorded by Diod. 16. 91-4, and therefore assassination? The basic story is retold here:

It was on the occasion of the marriage of Cleopatra to her uncle Alexander, the King of the Molossians. This was at Aigai in October 336 coinciding with the great religious festival and was almost certainly a countermeasure against Olympias' pleas to her brother to support her against Cleopatra-E. King Alexander, already Philip's brother-in-law through Olympias, now became Philip's son-in-law. Thus Philip would have had no further need of his marriage alliance via Olympias to maintain security on his western border, something he needed to be assured of before his departure into Asia with the main invasion force which was imminent. It is telling that Philip re-named Cleopatra-E

"Eurydike", the name of the dynastic queen-mother. Further, he had named their son "Karanos", traditionally the name of the founder of the dynasty.

The climax of the festival was a gathering in the theatre at sunrise, starting with a procession. Statues of the 12 Olympian Gods were to be carried in, followed by a statue of King Philip(2). A large number of foreign representatives were present (from neighbouring Greek city-states and alliances) in addition to the leading Macedonians gathered for the event. Once the statues were in place, Philip entered the theatre alone, supposedly to show that he did not need his guard around him to stay safe among his own people (he originally intended to enter with the two Alexanders, but changed his mind at the last minute and sent them ahead). Obviously, with hindsight, this seems a *big* mistake. For the moment, we will assume that this was a rare occurrence and therefore, for someone who wanted to kill him, a chance not to be missed(3). His Bodyguard, which included Pausanias-1, entered at a distance behind him and fanned out into their usual formation.

Alexander III and the King's Friends were already seated in the theatre, Alexander III presumably close to, or next to, the empty throne in the centre of the front row. At such a sensitive time for him (the official replacement of his mother by another alliance), one can imagine him watching for anything, however slight, that might further threaten his position as the King's most likely heir. Others, too, must have been watching for any shift in this delicate power-balance between father and son.

As the King moved to "centre stage" to acknowledge the cheers of the crowd, Pausanias-1 rushed forward, stabbed him fatally(4) (or threw a spear which killed him) and then ran to make his escape (there were horses tethered closeby in readiness for his "getaway"). Three of the King's Bodyguard took off in pursuit - Perdiccas, Leonnatus and Attalos- while the other three rushed to the King's side. But it was too late. King Philip was already dead or dying. Alexander III's friends must have rallied to *his* side too, ready to fight if Alexander became threatened. For a moment, there must have been chaos, panic and a frantic scrambling to find a new order. But with no King, there was no "right" side to take. For a moment, all the possibilities were wide open, then either with great presence of mind, natural self-preserving instinct or certainty from a plan already formed, Alexander, son of Aeropos, stepped forward and hailed Alexander, son of Philip, as King. The Doors of the Possible swung closed and Alexander III became King of Macedon as he began to take charge.

The three members of the bodyguard returned with Pausanias-1's body - Leonnatus had thrown the spear which killed him.(5)

This, then, is an account pieced together from the ancient sources and papyri fragments.

Now to the hearsay for the motive: it was said that Philip had been Pausanias-1's lover when Pausanias-1 had been a Royal Page; that Pausanias-1 still loved the King, who had taken a new lover. Pausanias-1 had insulted this rival, and the young man, Pausanias-2, had in effect committed suicide because of it. Feeling that Pausanias-1 had been the cause of the young man's death, the youth's relatives had revenged themselves on Pausanias-1 by getting him drunk and having him assaulted by stable boys. Pausanias-1 had asked for justice from Philip against the youth's relatives, but as the most powerful of them happened to be Philip's new uncle-in-law, Attalus (also noted as father-in-law), or maybe because Philip thought that justice had already been served, Pausanias-1's plea went unanswered. It was felt that Pausanias-1 must have nursed his wrong, until he saw Philip as the cause of all his misery and came to believe that only Philip's death would satisfy his need for revenge. (The code of exacting revenge for a wrong, supposed or real, was very closely related to a Macedonian's sense of personal pride or self-worth.)

This is the generally believed reason for Pausanias-1's murder of Philip. From here, things become even more shadowy. There are several possible motives. We present them here:

Ancient sources cite several possibilities: that Olympias turned Pausanias-1's mind to think of Philip as his real enemy (she could offer him sanctuary in Epiros); that the King of Persia wanted Philip destroyed (because he had sent the vanguard of an invasion force into Asia) and had sent agents to seek out an assassin (finding Pausanias-1 willing enough, they had offered him money and a sanctuary in Persia); that Alexander had asked for Pausanias-1 to kill "bridegiver, bridegroom and bride" meaning Attalus, Philip *and* Cleopatra-E, his father's love-bride, and the reason for his and Olympias' quarrel with Philip the year before.

To examine the death, we had to look at numerous factors, including the following:

1. Pausanius-2 either extracted a promise from Attalus, Philip's uncle-in-law, before death that Attalus would avenge his death, or blood-ties called for vengance. Philip could *not* resolve the matter to Pausanias-1's satisfaction without creating chaos in his own new family. Philip being

Philip, it is also rather likely that he simply did not feel the event warranted much on his part. After all, Pausanias-1 had indirectly caused the death of Pausanias-2, whose family had a right to avenge the death.

2. Pausanias-1 was devastated in every way. It was not only the physical assault that mattered, but that the ruination of his reputation and character had been completed. Being the paramour of a king was a far cry from being used by soldiers, servants or stablehands. It is important to remember that Pausanias-1 was one of the aristo and a Bodyguard of the King...thus, the event could have left him bitter and open to manipulation. Desperate men take desperate measures...

3. Attalus was related to Parmenion via a marriage either between himself and one of Parmenion's daughters, or between a relative (Attalos?) and Parmenion's daughter.

4. It is possible that Attalos the Bodyguard was a son or nephew of Attalus the General, since there seems to be confusion over this person or persons. Parmenion and Attalus were supposedly in Asia Minor at the time of Philip's death, so the Bodyguard and the general could not have been the same man. Perdiccas was a brother-in-law to Attalos. Normally, had he been related to General Attalus by marriage, he, too, would have been executed when Attalus was condemned. But this did not happen, which leads to further speculation..

5. Thus, Philip was related via marriage ties to Attalus, and Attalus was related via marriage ties to Parmenion.

6. Antipatros, Philip's chief advisor up to now, and his faction disliked and distrusted the Attalus-Parmenion-Philip alliance that was developing. In Macedon, factions were common and to see one faction seeming to be raised above another was a clear danger sign that a major power shift was about to occur.

7. Leonnatus and Perdiccas did not support the A-P-P alliance, as they themselves were from collateral royal branches. Also, Perdiccas was already aligning himself with Olympias, though this would not become apparent for years, and Leonnatus had a personal dispute with Philip. Both of these men were aligned with factions that opposed the A-P-P alliance.

8. Olympias(6) had a dispute with the A-P-P alliance. Naming Cleopatra-E "Eurydike" had placed her above Olympias as next in line to be Queen Mother. Naming Cleopatra-E's son "Karanos" after the founder of their dynasty had implications for Alexander. Whether or not Philip meant to create suspicion, he had done just that. Further, Philip had upset her plans

to enlist her brothers aid in this affair by offering Alexander of Molossia the hand of Cleopatra in marriage.

9. Both Attalus and Parmenion opposed Alexander's succession at this time(7). It could be they opposed the idea of a "non-Macedonian" on the throne; more likely they foresaw a time when they would hold the majority of power, had Cleopatra-E and her son lived.

10. It is highly unlikely Alexander would commit patricide. In the religions of the day, belief in the awful punishment that followed the patricide was very real. The "Kindly Ones", also called "The Sisters", would not forgive patricide. The Assembly could not have allowed a possible patricide to become King. There would not have been enough support to overcome the accusation, since several factions opposed his succession for numerous reasons.

11. Attalus was later convicted of conspiring in the assassination/ murder; Parmenion was also suspect but "acquitted" himself by turning Attalus over to be executed, thus "proving" his loyalty. It could be argued that Attalus had master-minded the entire affair, hoping to see the end of Philip and then the end of Alexander, thus putting himself in a powerful position as Regent to the infant Karanos, but that is another thought...that Alexander did not enter the theatre with his father may have thwarted plans for a double or triple assassination.(8)

12. Heromenes, Alexander and Arrhabaeus, sons of Aeropus, were also opposed to the A-P-P alliance, since it put them further away from the throne.

To find the likeliest truth, we started with Pausanias. Whether or not he had a personal motive for killing the King, we can presume he wanted to kill the king and *survive*, since he had "getaway" horses and ran from the scene. To do this, he would *have* to get out of Macedon; after all he was well-known, he could not have stayed and lived. The Army would have demanded his death as just punishment for killing their *elected* leader. (An act against the King was an act against the Macedonian People for the King was the personal embodiment of the People's will.)

Looking at the factions above, several scenarios were possible:

Imagine you are Pausanias - you hate the King and want to kill him, but you don't want to die. Olympias contacts you and promises you safety in Epiros. Epiros isn't too far away, you could probably make it to Epiros, but would you be safe there? If Alexander survived to become King, he would be bound by personal honour and by his oath as King to avenge Philip's murder. If he were not King but simply survived, he would still be bound by personal honour to avenge his father's death, and he would probably be seeking sanctuary in Epiros himself. Would Olympias protect you against *Alexander,* her son? *Could* she protect you against Alexander if Alexander really wanted to kill you? Not a good bet, so even if Olympias tempted you, you'd probably not accept.

But now, supposing that *Alexander III* had approached you to kill his father. Knowing Macedonian law and honour and Alexander, and the fact that if Alexander let you live *after* killing his father, Alexander *himself* would be dishonoured, would you say "Yes"? Not likely! Also, even though you are angry with Philip, you might reason that, to restore your honour and gain favour in Philip's eyes, you can now go to Philip and tell him that Alexander has tried to bribe you to kill him. Philip will see you in a new light, your honour will be restored; Philip will be very grateful to you for exposing the treacherous nature of his son. And if Philip *is* considering ridding himself of Alexander III and Olympias, you have handed him the perfect tool.

If agents from Persia heard rumour of your discontent, they might be tempted to approach you. Your first question would be "*From whom and how* did you hear this rumour?"- a very important question! The agents from Persia hint that if you kill King Philip, the Persian King would be very generous in his appreciation of your loyal act to someone who, after all, could be considered your true King (historically). You would know the Persian King has riches and power beyond belief. Persia is a *long* way from Macedon. Lots of Greeks are there as mercenaries and are doing very well for themselves. Alexander would NOT be able to reach you there. Even if he became King, he couldn't possibly defeat the might of the whole Persian Empire. Looks like a good bet, this one. You'd probably accept the Persian gold and think yourself on the way to a fortunate future- if- and it's a big IF, you can discover the answer to your first question! From that question all others will follow...

It is unlikely that Athens was involved, at least directly. It is suspected, however, that some rumour of a possible plot had gotten around. The Athenian representative made sure to announce that anyone who harmed Philip would *not* be made welcome in Athens (this alone would have made me start to look around!); plus, Pausanias would know he would not be able to hide anywhere *but* the Persian empire. Athens was not a "safe house" for Macedonian traitors.

Now, supposing some fellow Macedonians approach you. They are sympathetic, they understand what has happened and your disaffection. They are, moreover, very highly placed. They have had some time to become acquainted with you, to discuss where Philip is headed, what the future appears to be turning into: with the A-P-P alliance firmly in place, it is clear that the power and influence of some factions are on the wane, the threat of war could lead to both Philip and Alexander dying, and who, then, becomes the power at the throne?

Now, of course, human actions are inexplicable and often go totally contrary to anything we might suppose or invent. And considering the factors, it is almost more reasonable to ask who *didn't* either want Philip dead, or know about a plot to kill him! But looking at the end results helps in analyzing the possibilities.

From a papyrus fragment, we have some knowledge of the outcome of the trial of those present at Philip's murder. *Everyone* present was considered a possible suspect by the Macedonian Assembly and needed to be cleared by them, including Alexander III. This was their verdict (as much as we have of it): those in the theatre and the King's attendants were **not guilty** (thus they found Alexander "not guilty"). The diviner was crucified for reading the omens as favourable for Philip and thereby not warning him that something *very bad* was about to happen. Two sons of Aeropos (Heromenes and Arrhabaeus) - interestingly, their brother, Alexander, was first to proclaim Alexander III as King - were found guilty of conspiring with Pausanias and were executed. Pausanias's body was crucified. Heromenes and Arrhabaeus were killed sacrificially, along with the "getaway" horses who were also deemed guilty for their part in the murder of the King. Attalus, who was in Asia Minor with Parmenion, was found guilty of conspiracy and condemned, but was murdered before he could be executed.

Leonnatus and Perdiccas, though found "not guilty", were demoted from the Bodyguard and were not re-instated until much later.(9) Parmenion was given a position close to Alexander as an advisor and general, but this was probably based on an adage similar to "Keep your friends close, your enemies closer".

From the preceding information, we offer a possible scenario: Parmenion and Attalus, in Asia Minor, were approached by Persian agents. Neither of these men particularly supported some of Philip's foreign policies, and neither was known to support Alexander. They may have then covertly aided Persian agents in contacting the sons of Aeropus, who were promised they would be supported, with Persian gold, as Regents to Karanos, Philip's son by Cleopatra-E. The sons of Aeropus would have been kept unaware that Attalus and Parmenion were involved in the actual coup attempt, but were probably told that, to avoid a Macedonian civil war, the Persian empire would then negotiate peace between the factions. The sons of Aeropus would believe that, with themselves as Regents and the "grandchild" of Attalus (and thus, Parmenion) on the throne, an alliance could be built between the most powerful factions. Enlisting the cooperation of Pausanias, under the guise of friendship, Heromenes and Arrhabaeus (and possibly Alexander, who quickly switched to the winning side and may even have testified against his own brothers to save his life) plotted the death of Philip. Attalus and Parmenion, in Asia Minor, probably believed themselves outside suspicion. They may have also felt that, in the event of failure, the sons of Aeropus would be found guilty and be executed, leaving no trail back to them and leaving the throne open for the taking. It is also likely that, had the plot succeeded as desired, Heromenes and Arrhabaeus would not have enjoyed the Regency for long, but would have conveniently died, leaving Attalus and Parmenion, in effect, to rule. When Attalus was condemned, Parmenion quickly switched sides and probably had Attalus killed to avoid any tales from getting out.

Based on the facts, we conclude that Philip was assassinated, killed in an attempt to bring about political change. The promise of Persian support for the whole plot, with collusion from inside the Macedonian empire, seems most likely. Aeropus' sons were of the Royal House of Macedon and could have ruled with Persian backing. They needed

Pausanias to get close enough to the King. The timing? Philip's death certainly prevented the immediate invasion of Persia. Alexander had to wait two years before the Kingdom of Macedon was secure and strong enough again to allow his departure for Asia.

That Alexander was found "not guilty" and then elected King may have thwarted hidden plans; this in turn probably led to a brief time of turmoil, as factions and loyalties shifted, policies were implemented and tracks were covered! It is interesting that, later, suspected conspiracies against Alexander involved some of the same people suspected in Philip's death. Power is, and will always be, the great Tempter; the men and women in the halls of power are not there because they are the sort who lack ambition.

Finally, without further facts, and with the known facts standing the way they are, it would be perverse and consistent with obvious personal bias against Alexander to insist that Alexander had anything to do with Philip's murder. We submit, therefore, that Alexander be found resoundingly "not guilty", thereby returning the same verdict as his own countrymen did, *who were there with him at the time.*

Sikander and Halil - 1999

Footnotes:

(1) Plutarch, Justin, Satyrus

(2) The significance of this to the non-Macedonian Greeks present is not really relevant. (Though after Philip's murder, they may well have considered it as hubris for which the Gods had struck him down and that Pausanias had merely been their instrument.)

(3) Considering who his murderer turned out to be, that is one of THE Bodyguard, one of the seven most trusted men in the kingdom who traditionally guarded the King, we can only wonder why someone who had a daily opportunity to kill him with less risk to themselves choose such a public occasion to carry out the deed. Maybe the time was all important to the statement the killer was making.

(4) From archaeological evidence, it is believed that the murder weapon was a spear.

(5) For this, Leonnatus was demoted from the Bodyguard and was not reinstated for some years. Maybe he was mistrusted by Alexander as having silenced Pausanias to cover up a deeper plot. If Alexander could have been implicated by Pausanias, then surely Alexander would have not have punishedLeonnatus for his action, but would have rewarded him instead - incidental proof, if needed, of Alexander's innocence.

(6) Olympias herself had too much to lose should Philip die; considered non-Macedonian, without Alexander as King she would be just another target on someone's road to the throne. And Alexander's and her own insecure position with Attalus and Parmenion and their factions would place her life in jeopardy. Olympias had probably hoped to enlist her brother's aid in forcing Philip to acknowledge Alexander publicly as his heir and her as Queen Mother, but this was dashed when her brother accepted Philip's offer of marriage to Cleopatra. Since Olympias was on a weakened base at the time of Philip's death, we dismissed the theory that she instigated Pausanias's act.

(7) Attalus had declared himself Alexander III's enemy the previous year when he called Alexander's legitimacy into question.

(8) There were two "getaway" horses. Either Pausanias planned a very hard ride, or there were to be two assassinations that day- Philip *and* Alexander. When Philip changed the processional plans, he inadvertently affected the assassination plot. It's likely that Pausanius and Attalos were the assigned killers; Attalos decided against action when Philip changed the entry plan, Pausanius responded to the moment.

(9) We believe the death of Pausanias to be an accident. Though we feel Attalos had every intention of seeing him dead, it was Leonnatus who actually killed him - but we feel Leonnatus intended to cripple, not kill. That the spear hit as Pausanias fell, thus striking higher than we believe Leonnatus intended, was a fluke - but a fluke that allowed a number of conspirators to escape detection and punishment.

CHAPTER XVI

Religion

1. Divinity

Oracle of the Siwa Oasis

Entrance to the ruined Siwa Temple (2003), Egypt; walking in the footsteps of Alexander. Courtesy of Marcus Pailing.

In the winter of 332/331 B.C. Alexander made an 1100 kilometer detour in Egypt to pay a visit to the famous oracle of Siwa, situated in an oasis deep in the Libyan desert. Probably on November 14th of 332 B.C. Alexander was crowned Pharaoh of Egypt in Memphis, close to what is the present day capital of Egypt, Cairo. On April 7th of 331 B.C. Alexander was back to establish Alexandria on the Egyptian coast, the future metropolis of the Hellenistic world (although both Arrian and Plutarch record the foundation of Alexandria before the Siwa episode.) Anyway, the journey to Siwa must have happened somewhere in between those dates.

Maybe the enthronement as Pharaoh had already included divine honours to Alexander. Persian rule in Egypt - in a strange contradiction to the perception of Persian control over most other nations - might have been considered as oppressive and might have included the desacration of Egyptian holy shrines. The popular image of Alexander being welcomed as the liberator of Egypt, although Arrian limits this 'friendliness' to the Persian governor Mazaces, could be rather realistic. The whole country of Egypt fell into Alexander's hands without a single blow anyway. All our sources state that, after becoming master of Egypt, Alexander felt a strong urge (or 'pothos' if you like) to visit the oracle at Siwa.

The Siwa oasis was then called Ammonium or Hammon, its inhabitants Hammonii. It was considered to be one of the three great oracles in the ancient world, together with Delphi and Dodona (both in present day Greece). The priests of these oracles stayed in contact with each other. Especially during the Persian reign, this contact might have been quite valuable for the Siwah priests. Within the polytheistic view, there were little problems identifying the Egyptian Ammon, the Greek Zeus or the Roman Jupiter as one and the same deity.

Arrian's Account

Arrian explicitly tells us that Alexander found himself "passionately eager" to visit Siwa. Arrian refers to the tales of Perseus and Hercules, who were also believed to have ventured there, and suggests that Alexander must have had the ambition to equal himself to those mythological heroes. From present day Mersa Matruh Alexander ventured inland, accompanied by lavish rains in what was otherwise a dry and barren desert. Arrian also writes that two snakes - or two crows - were guiding Alexander and his army group inland. Because of these phenomena, he writes, he has no doubts whatever about the divine guidance of this mission.

Arrian gives a very brief summary of what actually happened when Alexander finally reached Siwah. He mentions a strange spring in the oasis: the spring water is hot during the night, cold during the day. Then he continues to say that Alexander visited the oracle and got the answers that his heart desired. That is it. Nothing more to say.

Diodorus' Account

Diodurus' story is perhaps the most vivid and entertaining account of Alexander's visit to Siwa. Diodorus talks of sudden thunderstorms, relieving Alexander's party from great thirst, and acclaims that this was a matter of divine providence. After that, we have crows guiding the army further inland. We have a description of the same spring as is mentioned by Arrian. But what is most entertaining about Diodorus, is his direct quotation of speech between Alexander and the Siwa priests.

Diodorus states that the god is represented by an image of emeralds and precious stones, which was placed on a golden boat and carried around by eighty (80!) priests. The boat is said to have moved by itself, not directed by the movement of the priests, but in fact directing the priests. There is 'speech' coming from the boat, but it is not clear whether this is actual speech or an interpretation of the movements made by the object.

Alexander aknowledges the shrine as his father, and then asks if he will indeed one day rule the whole earth. The oracle confirms this. Then Alexander asks if all the murderers of his father have been punished. Quite a stupid question, considering the situation. Subsequently the priests who interpret the answers of the god cry out loud: his real father can not be harmed by anyone, but if by chance he was referring to the mortal called Philip he should rest assured that everybody involved already has payed his penalty. After this Alexander honours the god with great gifts and returns to Egypt.

Curtius Rufus' Account

Our great source Quintus Curtius Rufus, probably the most cynical of all accounts we have, speaks of Alexander's "overwhelming desire" to visit Siwa and also of the unsual rains that facilitated Alexander's journey inland. "Whether as a gift from the gods or pure chance", Curtius writes. Again, animals (crows) are guiding Alexander through the desert.

Curtius mentions the same strange spring, with shifting temperatures opposed to the daytime sequence, and then describes the image of the god: a navel imbedded with emeralds and other jewels. The priests of Ammon address Alexander as 'son' (of Zeus, Ammon, Jupiter) and Alexander willingly accepts this title. They confirm that Alexander will rule over the world and that all murderers of Philip have already been punished. Curtius has Alexander's companions consulting the oracle as well: the oracle confirms that the god would think it is okay when they would bestow divine honours upon Alexander.

Plutarch's and Justin's Accounts

Plutarch records the same hardships for Alexander's party of getting to Siwa, but tells us it was primarily his "passion for surmounting obstacles" that made him complete the journey. Still Plutarch mentions divine assistance in the form of strange rainfall and ravens, but says that these events are in any case still more credible than the actual prophecy of the oracle. Again, in Plutarch, the Ammonic priests welcome Alexander as a 'son' and again Alexander asks the oracle if all of his father's assassins have been punished. "At this the high priest commanded him to speak more carefully", writes Plutarch.

Plutarch summarizes the event with a reflection on Alexander's behavior afterwards. When pierced by an arrow (probably in the Mallian town, India) he is to have said: "What you see here is blood, and not the ichor which flows in the veins of immortals." In the end, says Plutarch, Alexander did not allow himself to become foolishly overconfident because of his alleged divinity, but merely used it as a tool to impress others.

And finally there is Justin's account, brief as always, who states that Alexander was delighted that the 'Hammon' priests confirmed his divine origins. Alexander then goes on asking the same irrelevant question about 'his father's murderers' and his third question is answered by confirming that he will indeed once rule the entire world. Just as happened according to Curtius, his friends are told by the oracle that it is alright to venerate Alexander as a god rather than as a mortal king.

Overview

There is little evidence in the texts of our sources that after Siwa Alexander himself hold a firm believe in his divinity. It is true that he experimented with the Persian custom of *proskinesis* while in eastern Iran. But *proskinesis* was an honour traditionally bestowed on Persian kings, who although being elevated above the masses were never considered to have been conceived by a god. *Proskinesis* was quite modest too: it was nothing like throwing oneself on the floor in utter reverance, but a rather subtile gesture of a symbolic kiss while bowing the head in a humble way.

It is also true Alexander demanded that divine honours should be payed to him. Curtius Rufus - in a passage where he evaluates Alexander's enitire character - observes that the king reacted with excessive anger when someone refused to worship him. Arrian mentiones delegates from Greece, wearing laurel wreaths, visiting Alexander a few days before his death. The wreaths are evidence that the Greeks apparently had accepted Alexander's divinity. Whether Alexander had ever sent an official request to the Greeks to do so, is still disputed.

In Greek mythology there are generally three classes of beings: gods, men and heroes. Heroes distinguish themselves from ordinary men because, although mortal, they have supernatural origins somehow - a kind of hybrid between homo sapiens and immortal presences. Achilles was the son of the hero Peleus and the nymph Thetis. Hercules was the son of Zeus and the princess Alcmene. Perseus was the son of Zeus and the princess Danaë (her pregnancy was the result of a 'golden shower' from the god). If anything, what happened at Siwa elevated Alexander not to the level of a deity, but to the familiar concept - in Hellenic cultures that is - of a hero. In fact, the last and final hero of Antiquity.

It is very hard to put the entire matter in better words than our predecessors, who tried to understand the nature of Alexander too, already did twenty centuries ago. The best phrase might come from Quintus Curtius Rufus. Quote: "So Alexander did not just permit but actually ordered the title 'Jupiter's son' to be accorded to himself, and while he wanted such a title to add lustre to his achievements he really detracted from them." End quote.

Personal Observations

I had the privilege - though it is already long ago - to visit Siwa back in 1988. Siwa is still a delightful place and a beautiful oasis, quite a tranquil refuge from the hustle and bustle of most Egyptian cities. There is still that strange well, called 'Cleopatra's bath' nowadays, with crystal clear blue waters rising from deep beneath the desert sands and the most likely candidate for that "Water of the Sun" mentioned by our sources. (I swam in it, for the record.) However, time has gone by and there is no specific site or excavation connected to the alleged temple of the oracle of Zeus-Ammon. Those who are looking for a glimpse of Alexander's presence here, will find little or nothing.

2. Holy Koran

One of the most beautiful and poetic passages about Alexander the Great is found in the Holy Koran. The Koran refers to Alexander as Dhul-Qarnain (also spelled Zhul-Qarnain or Zulkarnein), meaning 'The Lord with the Horns'. To appreciate this passage, you might like to have a basic idea of the structure of the Koran.

The Koran (or Quran) means 'The Recital'. The words of the Koran are the words of Allah (God) revealed to Mohammed through the angel Gabriel. Mohammed (570-632 AD) retold these revelations in public speeches, which were in turn recorded by scribes. This collection of speeches make up the 114 chapters or 'suras'.

Most suras refer to persons known to both Jews and Christians as well as Muslims: the stories of Adam, Abraham, Moses and many other prophets. Only sporadically a story is entirely retold. Most texts start with a brief reference, then concentrate on the interpretation: the final explanation of the story in God's own words. So the texts basically run: If people question you about Moses, tell them... ; When they ask you about Jesus, tell them... . It is clear that all of these stories were very well known to Mohammed's audience. There was just no need to retell them. It was the explanation which mattered.

The same is the case with Alexander. In the sura 'The Cave' the Koran reads: "They will ask you about Dhul-Qarnain. Say: I will give you an account of him." Thus, the Koran treats Alexander the Great in the same way as it treats Noah, Jesus, King Solomon and others.

What follows is an account - of roughly 300 words - which explains the nature of Alexander. In essence it is stressed that Alexander was an instrument in the hands of Allah. God deliberately bestowed him with great powers and the means to achieve everything.

First Alexander traveled west until he saw the sun setting in a pool of black mud. There, on Allah's command, he punished the wicked inhabitants and rewarded the righteous. Next he traveled east until he found peoples who were constantly exposed to the flaming rays of the sun. They recieved the same treatment by Alexander's hands.

Finally Alexander traveled to the land of the Two Mountains. The backward peoples of this region were harrassed by Gog and Magog: the forces of chaos and destruction. Between the Two Mountains Alexander built a wall of iron blocks, joining the blocks with molten copper or brass. Gog and Magog were not able to scale the wall nor could they destroy it.

The sura ends with the statement that Alexander's wall, which protects mankind against its foes, will continue to exist until the Day of Resurrection, when Allah will level it to dust.

(Though the identification of Dhul-Qarnain with Alexander the Great is supported by most mainstream Muslim scholars, other scholars might support very different viewpoints. It is also said Dhul-Qarnain actually refers to the Persian King Cyrus the Great, or to the legendary Babylonian King Gilgamesh.)

CHAPTER XVII

Sex

1. Hephaistion Amyntoros

(Hephaestion, or Hephaistion, son of Amyntor)

Curtius calls him "omnium amicorum carissimus" to the king: dearest of all the friends. Alexander himself named him "Philalexandros"--friend of Alexander--in contrast to his great rival, Craterus (Krateros), who was merely "Philobasileus"--friend of the king. By the time of his death in Ecbatana in 324 BCE (only eight months before Alexander's own) he was the second man in the empire (Chiliarch), married to the sister of Alexander's own wife.

He and Alexander were coevals, and had shared their education under Aristotle at Mieza. They may have known one another before that. He was not a great military leader, and Alexander seems to have kept him away from (important) commands in actual battle. But this does not make him the incompetent or sycophant which he has sometimes been painted. Curtius stresses that he had great freedom to speak his mind to the king. And snatches of evidence in the extant sources suggest his real gifts were diplomatic and logistical, not military. It would be wrong to dismiss him as unimportant, and unnecessary to assume him a mere yes-man in order to get along with the king. His skills and those of Alexander were complimentary, not competitive.

We know little about his looks or personality. He was tall and, apparently, handsome. He also seems to have had a reputation for both charm and quarrelsomeness by turns. Later speculation whispered that he and the king had been lovers. While this is nowhere stated plainly, it is entirely possible. Nonetheless, it would be *reductive* to characterise their relationship solely in this way. Our model of friendship is not consonant with theirs. Within these ancient societies where homoerotic desire was freely, sometimes emphatically, expressed, intense friendships might well develop a sexual expression even while that expression was not the focus of the friendship.

Perhaps in the end, Alexander's own name for Hephaistion is best: Philalexandros. And so he has been known down through history: dearest of all the friends of the great Alexander.

Jeanne Reames-Zimmerman

(The Pennsylvania State University)

Here is another piece on Hephaistion, by Pothos Forum member Fiona:

Hephaestion son of Amyntor was Alexander's closest friend (Curtius 3.12.16). A native of Pella (Arrian *Indica* 18), he shared Alexander's education and upbringing (Curtius 3.12.16), and probably served in the army from an early age. He was commander of the bodyguards (*somatophylakes*) at Gaugamela (Diodorus 17.61.3), where he was wounded, and was later appointed joint commander, with Cleitus, of the Companion Cavalry (Arrian 3.27.4). At the end of the Persian campaign, he was decorated for bravery and leadership (Arrian 7.5.6).

By the time of his death he was *Chiliarch* of the empire, Alexander's second-in-command in both military and political spheres (Photius 92).

His distinguished military career included various special missions. Some were diplomatic, such as the occasion when he selected a new king for Sidon (Curtius 4.1.16), and others related to engineering, such as when he and Perdiccas bridged the Indus (Arrian 4.23.59), or the construction of the new fort and harbour at Pattala (Arrian 6.18.1, 6.20.1).

Hephaestion's interests were not limited to the military and technical; he corresponded with the philosophers Aristotle and Xenocrates, (Diogenes Laertius, *Aristotle* 5) and actively supported Alexander in his attempts to integrate Greeks and Persians (Plutarch *Alexander* 55.1).

In all that Alexander undertook, Hephaistion was at his side, a man he trusted completely and one upon whom he increasingly relied. Towards the end of the Bactrian campaign, when Alexander had cause to divide his forces, it was Hephaistion to whom half were entrusted when the objectives were not clear-cut, and Alexander needed someone who would be able to do what he would have done himself (Arrian 4.22.58).

Such was Alexander's regard for Hephaestion, that when he and his officers took Persian brides, Hephaestion was given Drypetis, daughter of the former king Darius, and sister to Alexander's own bride, Stateira. Alexander stated that he wished for their children to be cousins (Arrian 7.4.29).

Their working partnership was strong, and there is evidence that Alexander saw Hephaestion as an *alter ego*. He was free to speak his mind to the king, and Alexander, for his part, trusted Hephaestion with his secrets (Curtius 3.12.17).

It's also entirely likely that they were lovers. None of the extant sources says so in so many words, but by the time those were written down, such a love was already being frowned upon (Horace *Epistles* 2, 1, 156). Nevertheless, several well-attested incidents suggest that this was indeed the case. For example, Alexander and Hephaestion publicly honoured their dead heroes, Achilles and Patroclus, at Troy (Arrian 1.12.1). Even more telling is Alexander's overwhelming grief at Hephaestion's death. He had to be dragged away from the body (Arrian 7.14.6), and he ordered the sacred fires extinguished, a thing which was normally only done on the death of the Great King himself (Diodorus 17.114.4).

Hephaestion died at Ecbatana in October 324, of a fever which had similarities to typhoid (Plutarch *Alexander* 72.2). His funeral was probably the most expensive in history (Arrian 7.15.5), and with the permission of the oracle at Siwa, he was honoured as a divine hero (Arrian 7.23.8). Many of the splendid monuments in his memory went uncompleted. Alexander was still planning them at the time of his own death, just eight months later (Arrian 7.23.10).

2. Alexander's Lovers

Our classic sources certainly do not describe Alexander the Great as a human being with a vibrant sexlife. As Plutarch writes: "He showed little interest in the pleasures of the senses and indulged in them only with great moderation" (Plut. 4). Plutarch adds that Alexander "thought it more worthy of a king to subdue his passions than to conquer his enemies" (Plut. 21). And Alexander is supposed to have commented that "it was sleep and sexual intercourse which more than anything else, reminded him that he was mortal" (Plut. 22).

So if you are looking for raunchy details, you would be better served reading other literature than Alexander's histories. Plutarch recalls two events during which a few extremely handsome young boys were offered to Alexander as presents (as 'pets' obviously). Alexander reacts furiously on both occasions. He referred to the suggested loverboys as "debased creatures" and "sharply rebuked" the men who offered them (Plut. 22).

Of those Oriental ladies that were captured during his campaigns he is supposed to have said that "these Persian women are a torment for our eyes" and Alexander "was determined to make such a show of his chastity and self-control" that he treated these exotic beauties as "lifeless images cut out of stone" (Plut. 21).

Still, in our modern view, Alexander's moderate appetites provide some quite controversial elements. He had one mistress, three wives, one lifelong homo-erotic lover and a sexual relationship with a eunuch (a castrated man). And perhaps one or two additional one-night stands. If you are puzzled by the Ancient morals regarding passion, I would suggest that you read Jeanne Reames-Zimmerman's excellent pothos.org-article on Sexuality. You might also be happy reading the first chapter of Simon Goldhill's book Love, Sex & Tragedy. For an overview of the women involved in Alexander's career nobody can beat Beth Carney's Women and Monarchy in Macedonia.

Callixena

According to our Ancient source Athenaeus, Alexander's parents King Philip and Queen Olympias were concerned about young Alexander's lack of sexual desires and so they arranged for the Thessalian prostitute Callixena to entertain him. Callixena was reknowned for her beauty. Still, apparently, nothing happened. "Olympias often begged him to have sex with Callixena", says Athenaeus. Great parents, aren't they? See: Historical Sources in Translation, by Heckel & Yardley, page 39/40.

Campaspe

She is also known as **Pancaste**. Although she does never appear in the five major sources, modern author Lane Fox traces her existance back to the Roman authors Pliny (Natural History), Lucian and Aelian (Varia Historia). Campaspe was a concubine of Alexander and a prominent citizen of Larisa in Thessaly (Central Greece). According to Aelian she might have been the first woman with whom Alexander had sexual intercourse.

Alexander ordered his painter Apelles, presumably the only artist to be allowed to paint his image, to do a nude painting of Campaspe. But Apelles fell in love with Campaspe during the job. "So Alexander gave him Campaspe as a present, the most generous gift of any patron and one which would remain a model for patronage and painters on through the Renaissance", writes Lane Fox. Or, as Bosworth says in his Conquest & Empire: "Apelles depicted Alexander with the thunderbolt of Zeus in the celebrated painting for the Artemisium in Ephesus, and he was handsomely rewarded for doing so".

Painter Apelles also used Campaspe as a model for his most celebrated painting of Aphrodite (Venus) "rising out of the sea". She was "wringing her hair, and the falling drops of water formed a transparent silver veil around her form". See: Perseus digital library.

Barsine

Barsine was a Persian noblewoman by birth. Plutarch claims that she was the only woman Alexander had sex with before his marriage to Roxane. She became part of Alexander's entourage when the Macedonian general Parmenion captured the Syrian city of Damascus after Alexander's victory at Issus in the last months of 333 BC. Barsine was part of the 'Damascus treasure' as she had been sent there by King Darius III prior to Issus. Modern authors differ in viewpoint whether Alexander's liaison with Barsine started just before or just after his visit to Egypt in 332 BC.

Barsine was a daughter of Artabazus, a high ranking Persian and probably the former satrap of Hellespontine Phrygia. Artabazus and his family lived in asylum at Philip's court in between 352 BC to 342 BC, so Barsine and Alexander might have known eachother since childhood. When her exile ended she married to Mentor of Rhodes, the foremost general of the Persian empire. After Mentor's death around 338 BC she married his brother Memnon, who was placed in command of the war by Darius after the battle at the Granicus. However, Memnon died in early 333 BC and Barsine became widowed once again. When she was captured in Damascus she was in her early twenties, as she is believed to have been of the same age as Alexander, and she might already have been the mother of four children.

Our sources claim that Parmenion encouraged the liaison between Alexander and Barsine. Her qualities, says Plutarch, made Alexander "the more willing [...] to form an attachment to a woman of such beauty and noble lineage" (Plut. 21). She bore him one child, Herakles, probably in the year 327 BC. Modern English has no proper word to denote the relationship between Barsine and Alexander: she was neither a mistress nor a concubine. Her position was that of a woman of the king, which included special status, prestige and some (political) influence without being the king's wife. That was perfectly acceptable to the conquered Persians. The best short biography of Barsine is in Carney's Women and Monarchy.

Queen Statira, wife of Darius

We enter a controversial area here. After the battle of Issus in the Fall of 333 BC Alexander captured Darius' Royal family, including his wife and sister Queen Statira. (It is known that King Darius and Queen Statira shared at least one parent.) Statira was acknowledged as the most beautiful woman in all of Asia and "surpassed by none of her generation in beauty" (Curt. 3.12), but Alexander prided himself for not violating her integrity. However, our sources maintain that she died in 331 BC just before the battle of Gaugamela and both Justin and Plutarch add that she died in "childbirth" or "after a miscarriage".

In his commentary on Justin's Epitome (p. 160/161) Waldemar Heckel sums it up: "Hence, the original purpose of the story that Alexander treated the Persian captives with respect was intended less as an illustration of his restraint (*continentia*) than as an attempt to pre-empt any scandal which might arise from the circumstances of the queen's death". About this "most beautiful princess of her time" Plutarch quotes Alexander's very own words: "It will be found not only that I have never seen nor wished to see Darius' wife, but that I have not even allowed her beauty to be mentioned in my presence" (Plut. 22).

However, Curtius claims that Alexander saw her once (Curt. 4.10) and Diodorus records a short conversation between them (Diod. 17.37). Curtius adds that on learning of Statira's death Alexander "was in need of receiving consolation rather than giving it". Alexander reacted like one of his own relatives passed away, says Curtius. And King Darius immediately assumed that Alexander was guilty of his wife's demise and suggested that the messenger Tyriotes who brought him the news be put under torture. We will never learn the entire truth about Alexander's affection towards Queen Statira; but even if it was not sexual at all (Arr. 4.20), his deep sorrow might justify her listing as a true love.

Thalestris, the Amazon Queen

She is also known as **Minythyia** or **Thalestria**. In Hyrcania, the southern coast of the Caspian Sea, Alexander was visited by this legendary Queen of the Amazons in the autumn of 330 BC. (But Plutarch suggests she and Alexander met later in 329 BC near the Iaxartes River in Central Asia.) Thalestris had traveled something between 200 and 600 miles to join Alexander. Our sources are not clear about the location of the dominion of the Amazons, except that it bordered somewhere at the Black Sea.

"The dress of the Amazons does not entirely cover the body", says Curtius. "The left side is bare to the breast [...] One breast is kept whole for feeding children of female sex and the right is cauterized". Thalestris' eyes examined Alexander's body, and found that it in no way matched his reputation, as Curtius continues. Still, wearing her full armour, she begged Alexander to conceive a child with her. They spent "thirteen days" together as a couple (Just. 12.3; Diod. 17.77), while Alexander was "serving her passion" although "the woman's passion for sex was greater than Alexander's" (Curt. 6.5).

Thalestris left when she thought she had finally conceived. But she didn't. Neither did this story convince our more critical sources. "Aristobulus, Chares the Royal usher, Ptolemy, Anticleides, Philo the Theban ad Philip of Theangela, and besides these Hecataeus of Eretria, Philip the Chaldician and Douris of Samos all maintain that this is a fiction", writes Plutarch. Most famous is the quote of Lysimachus, former Companion of Alexander and later King of Thrace, when this tale about Alexander was read aloud to him (Plut. 46): "And where was I when all this occurred?"

Bagoas, the eunuch

In Hyrcania, just around the same time as the legendary Amazon affair, Persian nobleman Nabarzanes surrendered to Alexander and presented him with a lavish gift, the beautiful eunuch Bagoas. Nabarzanes was one of the three murderers of King Darius III, but Bagoas succesfully pleaded with Alexander to pardon Nabarzanes for his crime. Our sources are quite explicit about Bagoas. He was "an exceptionally good looking eunuch in the flower of his youth. Darius had had a sexual relationship with him and presently Alexander did, too" (Curt. 6.5).

Bagoas stayed with Alexander throughout the eastern campaigns as he is mentioned by Arrian in the Indica and appears again in the main classic narratives around early 324 BC. Bagoas by now "had gained Alexander's affection through putting his body at his service". But the self-appointed Persian satrap Orsines failed to pay court to the eunuch as Orsines said that he refused to pay respects to "whores" and men "who allowed themselves to be sexually used as women". This leaves little over to our imagination, does it? Curtius describes Bagoas in terms like "unconsionable male whore" and tells us the eunuch continued scheming against Orsines even during times when he submitted himself "to the shame of the sexual act" (Curt. 10.1). Alexander had Orsines executed.

Plutarch confirms Alexander's relationship with the eunuch "whose lover he was" and tells us about one event in Gedrosia in late 325 BC when both of them were cheered by the army. "The Macedonians clapped in applause and loudly called for Alexander to kiss him, until eventually the king took him in his arms and gave him a kiss" (Plut. 67). Eunuchs were boys whose genitals were partly removed before puberty, so that their boyish looks would be preserved in adulthood as they were not likely to develop masculine secondary characteristics. There is a short article on eunuchs in the Biography section of gaugamela.com.

Euxenippus

Euxenippus was a boy "still very young and a favourite of Alexander's because he was in the prime of his youth" (Curt. 7.9). He is mentioned by Curtius as he was sent by Alexander on an embassy in 329 BC. Curtius compares him to Alexander's friend Hephaestion, saying that Euxenippus rivalled Hephaestion in beauty but lacked charm because he was less masculine. In his text Curtius calls Euxenippus a "conciliatus", meaning both friend and lover, and uses the Latin word for hare to describe his charms. This is a subtle Latin pun hinting at male lovers.

Roxane

Her Persian name **Roshanak** is usually believed to mean "little star". However, author Jona Lendering derives the meaning to a somewhat less spectacular "girl with the bright face". The image of Roxane as portrayed by Rosario Dawson in the 2004 Oliver Stone epic Alexander will no doubt frame our popular perception of her appearance and character in many years to come. Curtius says Alexander fancied Roxane as his "control over his appetites was weakening" (Curt. 8.4).

There is no doubt that Roxane was Alexander's first official wife. Our source Arrian writes: "She was a girl of marriable age" and "the men who took part in the campaign used to say she was the loveliest woman they had seen in Asia, with the one exception of Darius' wife. Alexander fell in love with her at sight" (Arr. 4.19). Though she was a captive, Alexander refused to take her into his bed before they were married. But modern scholars agree there were political motives behind the wedding too, as Alexander wanted to appease the Bactrian and Sogdian warlords who were opposing his rule. (Roxane was the daughter of Sogdian nobleman Oxyartes.)

The marriage took place in spring (or August) 327 BC. Roxane conceived one stillborn infant son from Alexander in 326 BC. She was again pregnant when Alexander died in June 323 BC (see: Children). Modern interpretations of her personality might differ from passive non-entity to cunning first lady. She murdered Alexander's second wife Statira together with her sister Drypetis, widow of Hephaestion, in summer 323 BC: "She was jealous of [...] Statira, whom she tricked into visiting her by means of a forged letter [...]. In this crime her accomplice was Perdiccas" (Plut. 77). On the other hand, in 320 BC Roxane was taken into custody by the Macedonian regent Antipater and she was murdered by his son Cassander around 310 BC. The best overview of her life is, again, in Carney's Women and Monarchy. Curtius writes about Alexander and Roxane: "The man who had looked with what were merely paternal feelings on the wife and the two unmarried daughters of Darius - and with these none but Roxane could be compared in looks - now fell in love with a young girl of humble pedigree [...]. Thus the ruler of Asia and Europe married a woman who [was] part of the entertainment at dinner" (Curt. 8.4).

Queen Cleophis

She might be also known as **Candace** (Alexander Romance). Here we enter the grey zone between reality and fiction once again. Cleophis was the beautiful queen of Massaga, an ancient capital (now in northern Pakistan, Swat Valley). According to our Latin source Justin Cleophis was "sleeping with" Alexander and subsequently bore him one son named Alexander (Just. 12.7). Curtius adds: "Whoever his father was" (Curt. 8.10). Interestingly, if the Cleophis story is true at all, this sexual escapade happened just within a year after the marriage with Roxane and also quite shortly after the birth of Barsine's son. See also: Children.

Princess Statira & Parysatis

Statira is also known in the sources as **Barsine** or **Arsinoë**. In February 324 BC Alexander ordered the famous mass wedding at Susa, southern Iran, where he married both Statira, daughther of former Great King Darius III (336-330 BC), als well as Parysatis, daughter of the last 'really great' Persian King Artaxerxes III (358-338 BC). Statira and her relatives had been left behind in Susa in late 331 BC while Alexander's victorious army had moved on. We have little evidence about Alexander's affection towards Statira, except for "paternal feelings" (Curt. 8.4). Statira and her sister Drypetis were murdered in 323 BC by Roxane who "threw the bodies into a well, and filled it up with earth" (Plut. 77). We have no clue about whatever happened to Alexander's third wife Parysatis. (Some scholars suggest that 'Drypetis' is Plutarch's error for 'Parysatis', as Roxane probably had no motive to eliminate Drypetis.)

Hephaestion

He is also known as **Hephaistion**. It seems not more than appropriate to end this list with the man who was presumably Alexander's greatest love of all --- and perhaps his one true love. Hephaestion was a boyhood friend of Alexander, they were about the same age and they had shared their education with Aristotle at the temple of the nymphs in Mieza. When Alexander arrived at Troy in 334 BC, he and Hephaestion payed homage to the tombs of Achilles and Patroclus, stressing the fact that their relationship was supposed to mirror that of the lover-warriors from Homerus' Iliad.

Alexander and Hephaestion used to read together the letters received by Alexander, even the confidential letters sent by the king's mother Olympias. "Alexander did not stop him. Instead he took off his ring and put the seal to Hephaestion's lips" (Plut. 39). Arrian writes that Alexander loved Hephaestion "better than all the world". When Hephaestion died in 324 BC in Ecbatana, Alexander "lay stretched on the corpse all day and the whole night too" (Arr. 7.14). According to Plutarch Alexander's grief was "uncontrollable". He had Hephaestion's physician crucified (or hanged). During the campaign against the Cossaeans in early 323 BC Alexander termed the enemy victims a "sacrifice to the spirit of Hephaestion".

Hephaestion's funeral took place in spring 323 BC after months of preparation and costed 10,000 talents (Plut. 72). This amount is equivalent to some 450,000 US $ at modern gold rates. (Diodorus claims it was 12,000 talents.)

Hephaestion was no great military tactician and he was withdrawn as a major cavalry commander after 328 BC. His prominent role in the empire might have depended fully on Alexander's affection. Dr. Jeanne Reames-Zimmerman is the leading scholar-expert on Hephaestion.

3. Alexander's Men

After some discussion on the Pothos Forum, it was felt it might be useful to include here all the references to Alexander's sexual life - whether with women or men. Because of copyright questions, it is not currently possible to include full quotations from the sources, merely the references themselves.

No attempt is made here to discuss the various characters, whether their very existence or the nature of their relationship with Alexander. See the "Lovers" article above for more information, the short biographies in the "Main Characters" and "Minor Characters" sections; or why not join the Forum and ask your own questions about the people who inhabited Alexander's life?

What follows is as complete a list of the references that we have compiled so far. If and when we uncover any more we will add them.

References compiled by Amyntoros (mainly) and Marcus (a bit).

Bagoas, the eunuch

Aelian, 3.23; Arrian, *Indica* 18.8; Athenaeus, *The Deipnosophists* 13.603a-b; Curtius, 6.5.22-23; Curtius, 10.1.22-38; Plutarch, *Alexander* 67.3-4; Plutarch, *Moralia* 65C–E

Euxenippus

Curtius, 7.9.19

Hephaistion

Aelian, 12.7; Arrian, 1.12.1; Arrian, 2.27.4; Arrian, 7.4.5; Curtius, 7.9.19; Diodorus, 17.107.6; Diogenes Laertius, 4.2.14; Diogenes Laertius, 5.1.27; Diogenes of Sinope, *Letters* 24; Lucian, *Herodotus or Aetion* Excerpt from Chapters 4–6; Lucian, *A Slip of the Tongue in Greeting* Excerpt from Chapters 6–11; Lucian, *The Dialogues of the Dead* 12 (14); Plutarch, *Alexander* 39.5; Plutarch, *Alexander* 47.5-7; Plutarch, *Moralia* 180D; Plutarch, *Moralia* 181D; Plutarch, *Moralia* 332F–333A; Plutarch, *Moralia* 337A; Plutarch, *Moralia* 339F–340A

On the visit to the tent of the female Persian captives

Arrian, 2.12.6-8; Curtius, 3.12.15-17; Diodorus, 17.37.4-6; Valerius Maximus, 4.7 ext. 2a

On the death of Hephaistion

Aelian, 7.8; Arrian, 7.14; Arrian, 7.16.8; Arrian, 7.23.6-8; Cornelius Nepos, *Eumenes* 2; Diodorus, 17.110.8; Diodorus, 17.114-115; Epictetus, 2.22.17–18; Justin, 12.12; Lucian, *Slander* 17–19; Plutarch, *Alexander* 72.1-3; Plutarch, *Eumenes* 1; Plutarch, *Pelopidas* 34

Miscellaneous – Male

Plutarch, *Alexander* 22.1-2; Plutarch, *Moralia* 1099C; Plutarch, *Moralia* 179D–181F

4. Alexander's Women

After some discussion on the Pothos Forum, it was felt it might be useful to include here all the references to Alexander's sexual life - whether with women or men. Because of copyright questions, it is not currently possible to include full quotations from the sources, merely the references themselves.

No attempt is made here to discuss the various characters, whether their very existence or the nature of their relationship with Alexander. See the "Lovers" article above for more information, the short biographies in the "Main Characters" and "Minor Characters" sections; or why not join the Forum and ask your own questions about the people who inhabited Alexander's life?

What follows is as complete a list of the references that we have compiled so far. If and when we uncover any more we will add them.

References compiled by Amyntoros (mainly) and Marcus (a bit).

Barsine
Arrian, 7.4.4-6; Curtius, 10.6.10-14; Justin, 11.10; Plutarch, *Alexander* 21.4; Plutarch, *Eumenes* 1

Callixeina

Athenaeus, *The Deipnosophists* 10.434f-435a

Campaspe

Aelian, *Varia Historia* 12.34; Lucian, *Essays in Portraiture* 7–8; Pliny, *Natural History* Excerpt from 35.84-97

Cleophis

Curtius, 8.10.33-36; Justin, 12.7; *Metz Epitome*, 45

Concubines

Athenaeus, *The Deipnosophists* 13.607f–608a; Curtius, 6.6.7-9; Diodorus, 17.77.4-7; Justin, 12.3

Roxane

Marriage
Itinerarium Alexandri, 44.(ci); Arrian, 4.19.4-6; Arrian, 4.20.4; Curtius, 8.4.21-30; Diodorus, 17 (*Table of contents*); Lucian, *Essays in Portraiture* 7–8; Lucian, *Herodotus or Aetion* 4–6; *Metz Epitome*, 28-31; Plutarch, *Alexander* 47.4; Plutarch, *Moralia* 338D; Strabo, *Geography* 11.11.4
Death of Roxane's first child
Metz Epitome 70
Roxane at the time of Alexander's death
Arrian, 7.27.3; Curtius, 10.6.8-14; Justin, 12.15; Plutarch, *Alexander* 77.4; Strabo, *Geography* Excerpt 32.1.8

Stateira, wife of Darius, and her daughter, Princess Stateira

The capture of Darius' mother, wife, and her two daughters

Itinerarium Alexandri, 14.(xxxv)-15.(xxxvi); *Itinerarium Alexandri*, 23.(lvii); Arrian, 2.11.9-10; Arrian, 2.12.3-8; Arrian, 4.19.6; Arrian, 4.20.1-3; Athenaeus, *The Deipnosophists* 13.603b-d; Aulus Gellius, *Attic Nights* 7.8.1-4; Curtius, 3.11.24-26; Curtius, 3.12.1-17; Curtius, 3.12.21-26; Diodorus, 17.37.3-38.7; Justin, 11.9; Plutarch, *Alexander* 21.1-3; Plutarch, *Alexander* 21.4-5; Plutarch, *Alexander* 22.3; Plutarch, *Moralia* 338 D-F; Plutarch, *Moralia* 522 A; Valerius Maximus, *Memorable Doings and Sayings* 4.7 ext.2a

On the death of Queen Stateira

Curtius, 4.10.18-24; Curtius, 4.10.29-34; Diodorus, 17.54.7; Justin, 11.12; Plutarch, *Alexander* 30

Alexander's marriage to Princess Stateira (and Parysatis)

Aelian, *Varia Historia* 8.7; Arrian, 7.4.4-8; Athenaeus, *The Deipnosophists* 12.538b; Diodorus, 17.107.6; Justin, 12.10; Plutarch, *Alexander* 70.2; Plutarch, *Moralia* 329D-F

Thais the Courtesan

Athenaeus, *The Deipnosophists* 13.576e; Curtius, 5.7.1-8; Diodorus, 17.72.1-6; Plutarch, *Alexander* 38.1-4

Thalestris, the Amazon Queen

Itinerarium Alexandri, 42.(xcv); Arrian, 4.15.1-5; Arrian, 7.13.2-6; Curtius, 6.5.24-32; Diodorus, 17.77.1-3; Justin, 12.3; Plutarch, *Alexander* 46.1-2; Strabo, *Geography* 11.5.3-4

Miscellaneous - Female

Frontinus, *Stratagems* 2.11.6; Plutarch, *Moralia* 179E; Plutarch, *Moralia* 180F; Plutarch, *Moralia* 760C–D; Plutarch, *Moralia* 818B–C

5. Alexander's Sexuality

Introduction

The study of homoeroticism in ancient Greece has been the subject of serious study for the past 20 years since Sir Kenneth Dover's groundbreaking (and still seminal) work, *Greek Homosexuality* (1978, now in a 1989 revised edition).

Other important work in monograph form includes Marilyn Skinner's *Sexuality in Greek and Roman Culture* (2004), James Davidson's *Courtesan's and Fishcakes: the Consuming Passions of Classical Athens* (1998), John Winkler's *The Constraints of Desire* (1990), and David Halperin's *100 Years of Homosexuality* (1990). Yet none of these mention Alexander much, if at all.

One study that did was Daniel Ogden's "Homosexuality and Warfare in Ancient Greece" from *Battle in Antiquity* (1996). Ogden's paper collected a wide variety of ancient citations for many Greek cultures, not just Athens, and gave due attention to variations on the Athenian model, particularly with regard to military practice --- all of which made it a very valuable contribution to the ongoing scholarly discussion. Nonetheless, I found his analysis of Alexander somewhat uncareful and would caution readers on that score.

My remarks here address particularly the nature of Alexander's relationship with his lifetime friend and chiliarch, Hephaistion Amyntoros. Despite Mary Renault's romanticized, fictional portrayal of Bagoas in The Persian Boy, it was Hephaistion who enjoyed Alexander's primary affective attachment --- this, regardless of any sexual involvement. Hephaistion, not any of Alexander's three wives, was the king's real "significant other". For more information on Hephaistion himself, please visit my website <u>Hephaistion - Philalexandros</u>.

Was Alexander the Great gay?

Let me turn to one of the "hot" modern questions about Alexander. Was Alexander the Great gay?

No. I say no, not because he had no relationships with men and boys but because our term "homosexual" and "gay" are inappropriate terms for antiquity. Some may feel this to be splitting hairs. It is not. Language shapes us and the way we see the world. The ancient Greeks had no word that corresponded quite to our term "homosexual" --- hence my preference for "homoerotic".

The problem is that people on both sides of the modern argument insist on looking at the question as if Alexander and Hephaistion lived now. But they didn't. They lived then. And they thought about it all differently from the way we do. Too many people insist on filtering facts through the beliefs and customs of their own society (or religion or political agenda), and don't see that people in other places and times really can think differently about very basic things, including sex.

In general, the model for homoerotic attachments in antiquity was that of elder *erastes* (lover, pursuer, and active participant) and younger *eromenos* (beloved, pursued and passive participant). Individuals did not switch roles as the mood struck, and at least in Athens, coeval partnerships were frowned on. This summarizes the widely accepted "Dover Model," also called the penetration model, and should disqualify Alexander and Hephaistion who, Curtius tells us (3.12.16), were coevals. [Note that *aetas* does not mean the exact same age, merely the same stage of life and for reasons I won't go into here, Hephaistion was probably the elder by a year or so.]

Yet the model above is a largely Athenian pattern based on *Athenian* evidence... And it's quite the mistake to assume that *Athenian* norms held true in other Greek city-states. Evidence suggests that in Macedonia, pairs could be coevals, particularly among the adolescent Royal Pages (Arr. 4.13.3). There was still likely a small age difference, and an *erastes-eromenos* pattern was apparently maintained. Nonetheless, it was possible for two young men of roughly the same age to be sexually involved without that attachment being frowned upon. Thus, an affair between Alexander and Hephaistion cannot disqualified, as a strict reading of Athenian model would suggest.

Women

In modern studies, Alexander has been both portrayed as homosexual, and defended from such "allegations". One side accepts a reputed disinterest in women, while the other tries to deny it. Neither gives proper attention to Alexander's circumstances or to the ancient social realities.

Alexander was on an extended campaign which kept him constantly moving. Furthermore, relationships between men and women in ancient Greece and Macedonia, particularly within the upper classes, differed radically from those of today, and the polygamy of the Macedonian royal house would have been different yet again from that of a private family in the Greek south. So the fact that Alexander's primary affective relationship might have been with another man is not only unsurprising, but perhaps predictable. [For Macedonian royal polygamy, see William Greenwalt's "Polygamy and Succession in Argead Macedonia", *Arethusa* 22 (1989) 19-45.]

Alexander had three wives (Roxane, Stateira, Parysatis) and perhaps two mistresses (Barsine, Pankaste/Kampaspe), and there is suggestion that he had occasional assignations as well. [Plut. *Mor.* 180f = 760c; it is amusing that it is Plutarch who relates this tale, despite that author's valiant attempt to paint Alexander as a paragon of Greek sexual morality in chapters 21-22 of the Alexander.]

The simple truth is that a liking for women need not be false in order of an equal liking for men to be true. As typical of his era and culture, Alexander seems to have liked both.

Hephaistion

Let us return now to the question of what involvement, if any, Alexander had with his life-long friend, Hephaistion.

Our three Greek historians (Arrian, Diodorus and Plutarch) never term him *erastes* or *eromenos*, only *philos* or *malista timomenos*. Alexander himself calls him *philalexandros* (friend of Alexander). Curtius and Justin use only *amicus*, never *amans*. The only implication of a sexual relationship or use of the term *eromenos* for Hephaistion occurs in late sources or those of dubious authorship. [Ael. *VH* 12.7, Epic. *Dis.* 2.12.17-18, Diog. *Epistles* 24, and Luc. *Dial. Dead* 397.]

So while we do have evidence that it was possible, in Macedonian society, for young boys of roughly the same age to form attachments to one another which included a sexual expression, there is no indisputable evidence for such an attachment between Alexander and Hephaistion.

The evidence that does exist is circumstantial only. Personally, I find it perfectly convincing, but I do think we must acknowledge that we cannot state with certainty that Alexander and Hephaistion were lovers, either as young men, or continuing throughout their lives.

Circumstantial Evidence

But let us turn to this circumstantial evidence. First, and perhaps most important, is the literary comparison made between their friendship and that of Achilles and Patroklos, which 4th century Greece assumed to have had a sexual side. [For mention of Achilles and Patroklos as lovers in material with which Alexander himself was probably familiar, see Pl. *Sym.* 180a, TGF F135-36 (Aeschylus' *Myrmiddons*), and Aesch. *Tim.* 1.141-42.]

The problem with this bit of circumstantial evidence is that we cannot be sure when the comparison came about. Was it used in Alexander's own lifetime by Alexander and Hephaistion themselves? Certainly Alexander cast himself as Achilles! But was Hephaistion also cast as Patroklos at the time, or was this done later by the poetasters?

Much depends on what one makes of Arrian's story (1.12.1) that Hephaistion laid a wreath on Patroklos' grave at Troy, as Alexander laid one on Achilles'. Arrian gives this as a *logomena* --- a mere story: "They say... ". The tale was not, apparently, found in Arrian's chief sources (Ptolemy and Aristobulos). It is difficult what, or how much, to make of it. Did Arrian include it as part of a complicated flattery for his patron, the emperor Hadrian (who, as we recall, loved the youth Antinoos)? Certainly, others in Alexander's train were compared to figures in the Achilles legend (most notably old Lysimakhos as Phoenix). As Cohen has pointed out, these Homeric tales were living reality to the Macedonians. [Ada Cohen, "Alexander and Achilles--Macedonians and 'Mycenaeans", in *The Ages of Homer: A Tribute to Emily Townsend Vermule* (1995).]

So while we need not let skepticism completely overwhelm us, I'm afraid the verdict on the veracity of the Achilles/Patroklos pastiche must remain "unknown."

Hephaistion's Significance

Perhaps a safer allusive comparison is found in Curtius (7.9.19) wherein a certain young Euxenippos is compared to Hephaistion and found wanting in virility. While Curtius' use of *conciliatum* does not have to mean "beloved," that seems to be the thrust of the passage (pun intended). Euxenippos was a pretty boy who had caught the king's eye. (Alexander would hardly be the first Macedonian king to have a fling with one of his Pages.) This makes the boy's comparison to Hephaistion particularly suggestive. Has the king's current *eromenos* been set beside his old flame and come off the worse for the comparison? I believe this passage makes far more sense if we assume a romantic affair at some point between Alexander and Hephaistion.

Finally, Hephaistion's death and Alexander's grief is, itself, an indication of Hephaistion's significance to the conqueror. If Alexander is understood to be mourning a spouse (or spouse-equivalent), the severe nature of his mourning is far more comprehensible --- and proves, in fact, not to be abnormal or pathological at all, contrary to much ancient and modern opinion. Yet, again, Alexander's bereavement is not proof of a sexual relationship between the two; it only proves, or at least suggests, that Hephaistion occupied the central emotional place in Alexander's life.

We must remember that the two of them had been friends at least nineteen years, if we accept Mieza as the *terminus ante quem* for their meeting. During much of this, they would have have lived in close quarters on campaign and no doubt seen one another daily when not away on independent missions. Nineteen years is longer than many modern marriages.

Whatever the truth of their sexual involvement, their emotional attachment has never been seriously questioned. In the *Nicomachean Ethics*, Aristotle speaks of the true friend as the "second self" (1170b) and postulates there is only one special friend (1171a). At least some of his teachings seem to have made an impression on his student! [For further comment on Alexander's bereavement, see now "The Mourning of Alexander the Great," *Syllecta Classica* 12 (2001) 98-145.]

Conclusion

Finally, I would like to point out that whatever one chooses to believe about Alexander's sexual relationship with Hephaistion, it would be quite reductive to characterize it solely as an affair of the gonads.

Greek philia included a level of friendship that was particularly intense, one which is sometimes difficult for us now to grasp. In our societies, friendship all too often exists on the boundaries of other relationships --- those with our family or lovers. For the Greeks, though, such was not the case, and perhaps they were richer for it.

In short, our models of friendship are not consonant with theirs, and in these ancient societies where homoerotic desire was freely, sometimes emphatically, expressed, intense friendship might well develop a sexual expression even while that expression was not the focus of the friendship, or even thought of as particularly characteristic of it.

Thus, it would be inappropriate to refer to the friend as "lover" except in very specific circumstances, as such would fall short of encompassing the whole. Alexander's choice of *philalexandros* for Hephaistion said far more about the nature of his affection than calling him merely *eromenos*.

Article submitted to pothos.org by Dr. Jeanne Reames-Zimmerman, Department of History, University of Nebraska at Omaha. © Dr. Jeanne Reames-Zimmerman.

The material here is based on "An Atypical Affair? Alexander the Great, Hephaistion, and the Nature of Their Relationship", by Dr. Jeanne Reames-Zimmerman, The Ancient History Bulletin 13.3 (1999) 81-96. The material may not be reproduced without permission from the author. This pothos.org article was fully revised on 17th December 2004.

Additional Note from the Author

I have found portions of this article very selectively quoted to support political or social positions that **I do not** support --- which, in fact, I may find disquieting. If such quotes are within fair-use rights, I can hardly forbid them. And it's not disagreement or differing opinion that disturbs me --- it's the use of my own words to justify modern political agendas with which I don't agree that disturbs me... Particularly when it's not made clear that **I don't** subscribe to them.

Homosexuality and gay rights are topics that evoke strong feelings. Therefore let me be **extremely clear** where I stand: I am in support of civil rights for gays and lesbians, up to and including marriage. Anti-gay writings that quote me in support of their positions **do not** reflect my own opinions, and I do not believe that current research into ancient Mediterranean sexuality is driven by a 'gay agenda'. Like any good historical research, it's driven by a quest for the truth, insofar as we can know it, and pursued by scholars of **all** affective-sexual orientations. By the same token, however, gay rights activists who would overdraw the parallel and claim Alexander as a gay hero, refusing to recognize differences between now and then, are equally without historic basis. Please allow the historic truth to be duly complicated, as it so often is.